Advance Praise

In *The PEACE Process*, Miriam extends the hand that will bring integrative practitioners forward into their own best success and, in so doing, will improve the lives of countless individuals. Her PEACE plan is comprehensive, practical, and founded upon her personal learnings and successes. Practitioners who create the focus and the will to follow her plan will not only achieve success, but perhaps even more importantly, will re-experience the love, excitement and passion with which they started their professional journeys.

Lise Alschuler, ND, FABNO
Past President, Oncology Association of Naturopathic Physicians
Co-author, *Definitive Guide to Cancer* and *Definitive Guide to Thriving After Cancer*
www.DrLise.net

As an integrative physician who has, through trial and error, created a very successful practice model, I can only say I *WISH* I could have had access to this book earlier! It would have shaved years off of my learning curve, saving me time, money and frustration. *The PEACE Process* gives a step-by-step framework to build a successful holistic practice and is a must-read for anyone wanting to succeed in our "well-care" industry.

Rebecca Hunton, MD
Medical Director
RHMD Radiantly Healthy
www.drhunton.com

Miriam's enthusiasm is irresistible. This illuminating and highly instructive book introduces marketing concepts that are essential for helping holistic practitioners reconnect with their passion, that underlying motivating force that builds a business by connecting people to people. Her stories and simple "how-to techniques" are compelling. If you want to grow your practice, this is your book.

Alex Holland, M.Ac., L.Ac.
Past President, Han University of Traditional Medicine
Author of *Voices of Qi: An Introductory Guide to Traditional Chinese Medicine*
www.hanuniversity.edu

There's no doubt that one of the biggest struggles for a healthcare practitioner is creating a healing, nurturing, and caring clinical practice, and at the same time ensuring that it is grounded, financially viable, and sustainable. These two paradigms can truly co-exist without guilt, shame, or fear. Zacharias shows the modern professional HOW to finesse the yin of their healing arts with the yang of everyday business and reality. Invest in following the PEACE Process and get sustainable results that can keep you surviving and thriving, doing what you love and feel called to do!

Deanna Minich, PhD, FACN, CNS,
Author and functional medicine nutritionist
www.foodandspirit.com

I've seen Miriam Zacharias in action. Her practice management seminars are inspiring; she wants you to optimize your outreach because she is an avid cheerleader for the natural medicine paradigm. In *The PEACE Process*, she beautifully encapsulates her practical formula for overcoming often self-imposed obstacles to success, so that practitioners can take tangible steps to fully realize their potential for healing.

Ronald L. Hoffman, MD, Certified Nutrition Specialist (CNS)
Medical Director, Hoffman Center, and host of the *Intelligent Medicine* radio show and podcast series
www.drhoffman.com

Having seen the impact of Miriam's passion and her PEACE Process on the many integrative practitioners she has lectured on Emerson's behalf, she is the perfect person to write a book on this topic. She'll help you get focused, find your niche market, and avoid the distractions that prevent your practice from meeting your needs AND those of your patients.

Andy Greenawalt
Past President and CEO, Emerson Ecologics
emersonecologics.com

Rather than stringing together a few pointers, *The PEACE Process* takes you firmly by the hand and methodically walks you through how to become a successful, purpose-driven entrepreneur. Written with insight and humor, and guided by years of real-world experience in the holistic healthcare community, Miriam passionately teaches the importance of really defining your niche, how to create your unique brand, how to utilize social media and other marketing tools to maximize your impact, and so much more... all while staying true to your deep-rooted purpose. *The PEACE Process* will teach holistic practitioners once and for all how to happily embrace marketing, attract more clients, and finally enjoy the "Power Practice" they richly deserve.

Jini Cicero, CSCS
Functional Medicine Consultant
www.jinifit.com

Every holistic health practitioner needs *The PEACE Process*. It lays out the path to success your business classes in school were supposed to provide. The principles of *The PEACE Process* provided us the courage to re-brand a boring, uninspiring generalist practice (which required tons of marketing) into a cohesive, specialist clinic. The haters came out and told us how foolish we were on social media and in person; however, after the storm, we added more followers, more new patients, and authority was ours.

Christopher Oswald, DC, CNS
Co-Founder, Hudson Headache
www.hudsonheadache.com

This is such an important book for integrative and holistic health practitioners. It provides the keys to business success that every practitioner needs but almost never gets in their pre- or even post-graduate training. Miriam got it right and made it an entertaining read, too! If you want to grow your practice and help more people, get this book.

Mike Katke
Past VP of Marketing, Designs for Health
Co-founder and former VP of Marketing, Metagenics, Inc.
Creator of the FirstLine Therapy
www.designsforhealth.com

As a new healer I really didn't know what to do to get my business started and I was very nervous about marketing. *The PEACE Process* helped allay my fears by setting out a very practical, step-by-step process for making decisions about my niche, product offerings, and marketing message with integrity and in a way that truly let me define who I am and what I bring to people to improve their lives. It is a must-read for any holistic practitioner.

Ann Keating MS, CNS, LDN
Nutritionist and Wellness Coach
www.annkeating.com

Miriam provides practical advice that every practitioner needs to hear, and will have you looking at your business and marketing through a new lens. That lens will help you identify the patients you actually WANT to see and hone your messaging and practice to bring them in your door and keep them. This is a must-read, and even more so a must-DO for any integrative healthcare provider.

Dr. Jaclyn Chasse, ND
Medical Director
www.northeastintegrative.com

If you are a holistic health practitioner, *The PEACE Process* will get you right between the eyes... in a good way. It will help you cut through the chatter, the hem and haw, and the "noise" that goes on in that head of yours. Entrepreneurship is a lonely place sometimes and Miriam provides you partnership and companionship on that isolated ship. Applying this process has allowed me to pour all of what I know into helping the previously unhelped. Practice is much easier when you are a true authority rather than just another generalist.

Corey Schuler, MS, DC, CNS, LN
metabolictreatmentcenter.com

As a former corporate sales and marketing guru, nutrition professional Miriam Zacharias skillfully inspires readers to find business clarity, utilize effective marketing strategies, attract prospective clients, and build a thriving holistic health-care practice. Mission accomplished! *The PEACE Process* should be standard text for every practitioner. Nutritionists, yoga teachers, chiropractors, fitness instructors, sales reps—*every* entrepreneur will benefit from this book.

Melissa McLean Jory, MNT
Co-author of *The Gluten-Free Edge: A Nutrition and Training Guide for Peak Athletic Performance and an Active Gluten-Free Life*
www.glutenfreeforgood.com

Miriam can teach you how to best develop your professional niche and magnetize potential clients to come on board. She can connect you with your passion and help you earn more than you thought possible—and with integrity and dignity.

Hyla Cass, MD
Author of *8 Weeks to Vibrant Health*
www.cassmd.com

This book will help the holistic entrepreneur get clear on where and how to start! With her straightforward method and direction, I was able to identify my niche, outline the "how and where" to begin, and successfully launch my business. Equally important, Miriam's approach to business keeps me connected to why I am doing this—my energy stays flowing so I can help those I want to serve. Any holistic entrepreneur will find *The PEACE Process* full of the vital details and guidance to create, launch, and have continued success in the business of their dreams.

Deborah Joy Gudelsky, MS Nutrition
Creator of Deborah Joy's Gluten Free
www.deborahjoysglutenfree.com

I call on holistic practitioners all day, every day. Many amazing practitioners are not so amazing when it comes to branding themselves and marketing their practices, and this is a leading cause of "practice mortality." Think of *The PEACE Process* as your "business bible," a reference guide that will instruct you, on every level, from novice to expert, on how to put your practice on the map, and send patients through your door, right to you. It is well written, emotionally impactful and has practical, applicable information that will improve your practice the moment you start applying it, in every single paragraph! Buy it, apply what you learn and you WILL be successful.

Ted Haun, LE, CCN
TLN Consultants, Inc.

I have listened to Miriam speak over the years and she is a wealth of information when it comes to marketing and branding. *The PEACE Process* provides the framework upon which you can and will succeed. Employing these strategies is one of the most powerful things I have done in creating a successful Functional and Integrative Medicine practice. I would highly recommend reading this book and working through the exercises that Miriam teaches, as it will help you figure out and focus on what is truly important.

Jill K. Valerius, MD, ABIHM, IFMCP, ATC
www.nowhealthpalmer.com

As president of our association, Miriam has been an integral part of teaching me and my team how to break away from the immobile perspectives of the past, and move us into a new and dynamic, purpose-filled marketing shift. With her help, our membership has *quadrupled* over the past seven years and continues to grow rapidly. This book is perfect for any practitioner who truly wants to grow their business in order to help and heal, and for any business owner who is ready to embrace phenomenal growth.

Nicole Hodson, NC, Board Certified in Holistic Nutrition
Executive Director, National Association of Nutrition Professionals
www.nanp.org

Holistic health practitioners can breathe a sigh of collective relief knowing that we have Miriam Zacharias in our corner! A rare bird, indeed, she brings genuine passion for whole-system healing (born of her own suffering in the allopathic medical system), bona fide experience in marketing, and firsthand experience as a holistic practitioner to the table. *The PEACE Process* not only inspires, it also validates the challenges and struggles we are likely to have, which is one of the first steps to moving past a block. Miriam offers very specific, doable tasks that can help us create a successful practice based on solid science but in a very readable format that will ensure this book will be by your bedside (or on your office desk) instead of collecting dust on a shelf.

Karen Olson, MA, LPC
Certified Imago Relationship Therapist
Owner of Caritas Center for Healing, specializing in holistic services for optimum health
caritashealing.com

The PEACE Process is an ideal guide for healthcare professionals who break out into hives whenever someone mentions the "M word." Marketing, as Miriam points out in this lively and readable book, is really a matter of clarifying your purpose and then communicating that purpose with enthusiasm. Packed with practical tips for re-discovering your "Why" and then projecting it via a wide range of media, *The PEACE Process* gives you the "nuts & bolts" guidance you'll need to build a thriving and flourishing integrative practice. Miriam combines her personal experience with her sharp business acumen to create an outstanding guide for any practitioner who envisions a practice focused on true healing, not just disease management. Highly recommended!

Erik Goldman, Editor
Holistic Primary Care
www.holisticprimarycare.net

I know more relevant information about marketing after reading *The PEACE Process* than I did after earning my MBA! Miriam combines a true understanding of the holistic practitioner's unique challenges with the strategies and tactics that really work to create a thriving healing practice. You'll appreciate her thorough step-by-step approach as she leads you through the entire process from defining your purpose (the "why") to attracting and keeping happy, repeat clients/patients. She demystifies marketing so we can get out of our own way and help more people, which is after all "why" we do this work.

Julie Spero, MBA, NC
Treasurer, National Association of Nutrition Professionals
Certified Nutrition Consultant and Nutritional Kinesiologist
www.eclecticwellness.com

Miriam has the uncanny ability to make you feel as if she is speaking directly to you. Once you start, you will not be able to put it down. She knows the challenges facing holistic health practitioners and understands their concerns so well, but more importantly, she knows how to overcome them. No complicated theory or conceptual clouds of confusion here, only a clear, precise, perfectly scaled, beautifully presented, personalized strategy. When you are finished, you will be amazed to see you have a comprehensive, multidimensional marketing strategy built entirely around you, your practice, and your niche... all wrapped up in a package that anyone can manage.

Carol L. Bysiek, MSW candidate
Certified Health Coach and former Fortune 500 executive
www.lilypadwellness.com

As a clinical practitioner my marketing activities must fit either into brief segments between patient appointments or at the end of the day. I find it difficult to determine how to best use these times. It's easy for me to get lost. Miriam has an amazing ability to help me gain focus and create momentum. She makes marketing concepts simple and immediately useable for the integrative health practitioner. In her book, *The PEACE Process,* she continually takes you out of "idea" mode and into fast action. I find Miriam's mixture of accountability and vision to be enlightening and inspiring. A powerful read for sure!

Cheri Jones, RD, MPH
The Jones Institute for Advanced Medicine
www.jonesinstituteusa.com

Miriam Zacharias's unique knowledge of marketing and the world of holistic health have been turned into a fun and compelling business book that serves up everything practitioners will need to thrive in today's wired world. Those who are searching for the practice marketing "bible" need to look no further than *The PEACE Process.*

Dianna Smith
Past Chief Marketing Officer, Natural Partners, Inc.
www.naturalpartners.com

If you are in the health care field, marketing your practice is often a difficult thing to do. Miriam has put together fabulous tips that will help you not only start the process of selling yourself but will give you the confidence to keep on doing it with style and integrity.

Marcelle Pick, OB-GYN and Pediatric Nurse Practitioner
Owner of Women to Women
Author of *The Core Balance Diet: Is It Me or My Adrenals, Is It Me or My Hormones*
Marcellepick.com
Womentowomen.com

Miriam provides outstanding information on how to enhance your visibility online to dramatically increase your audience and income. She has a great way of making all this information understandable and usable for those motivated to take their message to the masses.

Gregg Stern, DC, DACCP
Stern Chiropractic, Ltd.
www.SternChiro.com

THE PEACE PROCESS

*Attract a steady stream of clients
and create a thriving holistic practice*

by

Miriam G. Zacharias

Second Edition

Published by Black Point Publishing
ISBN-13: 978-0-9909130-1-6
Library of Congress Control Number: 2015900965
Printed in the United States of America
Editing by Gwen Hoffnagle

Dedication

To my big brother Eric, who wasn't too old to rock and roll,
but was way too young to die.

Contents

CONTENTS

Preface

It took a horrific tragedy to put my life on a new path.

In the early 1990s, life was sweet. I had a key role as a sales and marketing director at Microsoft Corporation running a two-billion-dollar business division and making great money. I had status, a beautiful home, lots of important customers, and very few worries.

One day I got the call from my dad. I'll never forget that moment. It was September 14th, 1994, when I heard his voice cracking across the phone line, "Honey, you need to come home. Eric is gone." Eric was my big brother, a super cool dude whom I adored. When I heard that he had died, I was mad as hell... but not terribly surprised.

Three years prior to his death, Eric had gone into the hospital—he was forty-three at the time—complaining of chest pains. After putting him on the treadmill, doctors scheduled bypass surgery for first thing the next morning.

During his operation something went terribly wrong. The surgeon walked into the waiting room and told my family, "We had a little problem in the OR, but everything is okay now, everything is fine, it's all fine." The surgeon's face was white as a sheet and his hands were trembling. My mom was an RN and knew that so many "fines" meant the exact opposite was true. She immediately called for the operating room records, and along with some of her doctor pals discovered that a dreadful mistake had been made.

Exhausted from performing back-to-back bypass procedures over the past who-knows-how-many hours, the surgeon had left the room during Eric's operation and relegated "finishing up" to one of his interns. The inexperienced intern connected a vein to an artery, which put Eric into cardiac arrest.

Miraculously Eric survived. But his problems were just beginning.

The surgical mistake destroyed 80 percent of his heart function, but that was only part of the story. For the next three years, my big brother was tortured by one affliction after another. While bedridden awaiting a new heart (his only chance for long-term survival), he developed shingles. Shortly after that, a hole in his esophagus. Hepatitis. Chronic bronchitis. And finally a brain abscess.

One month before he died, when Eric was admitted to the hospital for what turned out to be an inoperable brain tumor, a blood draw revealed yet another glaring medical blunder. When he had undergone the original heart surgery, he had been given seven units of blood. Four of the units were tainted with HIV and hepatitis. Eric died of AIDS as a result of receiving a dirty blood transfusion during the botched heart surgery three years prior. Wow. Talk about a lot to comprehend.

My brother's death crushed the family. My mom's health rapidly declined due to stress, insomnia, and depression, and she died not long after Eric had. The day she died was my last day at Microsoft. I was so angry that I pulled the plug on my career because selling one more box of Windows seemed pretty meaningless.

Shortly after my mom's death, my brother Marc had a "break with reality" and was institutionalized. Marc's psychiatrist told me that my brother was very sick and to never contact him again.

My dad, also a victim of an iatrogenic event, spent his final days bitter and angry with life. His final message to me involved a dismissive wave, shooing me out of his hospital room in disgust the day before he died.

I was all alone, pissed off, and wondering how to channel my rage.

My anger got me digging around in the field of health, and I made an amazing discovery: a healthy lifestyle could not only *prevent* disease but reverse it—including heart disease. Now that might seem obvious to you, but at that time it was mind-blowing to me. What I came to understand was that while Eric's life was destroyed by a couple of medical mishaps, he might have been able to avoid the hospital in the first place had he not indulged in excessive smoking; drinking; shaky dietary behaviors; long, sleepless nights of playing guitar in smoke-filled night clubs; and everything else that went along with his rock-and-roll lifestyle. That, I discovered, was the real tragedy in Eric's story.

I instantly enrolled in school to study holistic nutrition hoping to help others avoid this kind of misery. I had a decent baseline understanding of clinical nutrition from my master's program at Ohio State, but based on my recent insights I knew that a conventional dietetics program wasn't going to cut it.

After graduating and setting up shop as a holistic nutrition professional, I got busy helping people with their nagging lifestyle issues by teaching them some simple dietary shifts. It was amazing and hugely rewarding to see the theory work in action! During this period I also took on a large nutrition consulting project for a peer in the holistic health field. In addition to asking me to coach her clients to make progress with their health issues, she wanted me to help her build her brand and make an impact in her community using all the latest digital and in-person marketing strategies available. That made sense. After all, I had devoted my entire working life to sales and marketing. We were thrilled as we watched the size of her client list rapidly expand.

But something was wrong. I began to notice that my new peers and associates in the holistic health field were struggling financially. I loved my community; they were passionate and caring healers with big dreams—as big as those of my old leader, Bill Gates—only instead of a computer on every desk and in every home running Microsoft software, their dreams were to heal desperate people *safely and naturally*. It was killing me to see holistic health practitioners go broke and go back to their old, uninspiring jobs in order to pay their monthly bills.

Week after week I felt more restless. I had a burning new passion that was stirring inside me: I longed to switch gears and leverage my twenty-five years of sales and marketing experience with my success as a holistic nutrition professional and my love for healing into a brand-new role as a marketing advisor and teacher to the holistic health community. I figured that if I could help you be more successful, *countless* lives could be impacted—certainly way more than I could ever impact on my own as a clinician. I was on a mission to create an army of holistic and integrative health leaders. The clock was ticking; now was the time to change things up and bring my dream to fruition!

I told my client that I was moving on to follow my vision and build my new business. In response she said four words: "You're going to fail."

Those words stung like you wouldn't believe. After all, I had achieved great success throughout my life, and had certainly helped her grow her business. It didn't make any sense. Still, her opinion didn't matter at all; I was on a mission and nobody was going to stop me. *Ever.*

When I first stopped working with her, I had plenty of challenges in reinventing myself. Even after all my success in marketing, things just weren't happening fast enough. I had built a great website, gotten involved with social media, made videos, started a blog, you name it. And while I saw a steady trickle of clients, the going was painfully slow, and I was barely bringing in enough cash to cover my expenses. Who am I kidding? I wasn't covering anything—I was pilfering my personal financial assets to run my business.

More than once I thought about pulling the plug on my mission. I even started to send my resume out, but the thought of helping yet another company realize *their* dream at the expense of burying mine made me want to throw up. But I needed to generate income before I drained even more of my personal savings.

I was baffled. I was following all the steps that were necessary to build a thriving business, and I knew how to help holistic practitioners succeed. What was missing? Something was keeping me from seeing faster success in my work.

I had lost sight of my *purpose!*

In my haste to succeed I had become disconnected with the force that had shoved me out of my comfy corporate job and into the world of holistic health. I had ignored the nagging voice in my head that was screaming, "Go build your dream, Miriam!" I had allowed the influences and opinions of others, including those of my client, to pull me off center and poke holes in my will. I had let fear of the unknown and the difficult paralyze me. Like a ship without a rudder, I had lost my focus.

Suddenly an arrow of awareness shot straight through my heart! I immersed myself in myself, spending hours to the point of obsession learning how to reignite my fire. I finally asked myself the question, "At the end of my life, what one thing will I regret if I never accomplish it?" This single thought scared me to death. This became the most important question of all. It was visceral and troubling. I had to reach deep down into my soul and get back to my "why."

When I relaunched my business after reconnecting with my purpose, everything clicked. I no longer concerned myself with the naysayers or the doubters around me. I was laser-focused on my mission, and those who believed in that same vision were attracted to me, too. Soon I was being asked to speak at integrative medical conferences and lecture at esteemed institutions like Bastyr University. I became adjunct marketing instructor at Maryland University of Integrative Health, and faculty for the Heal Thy Practice conference, and created the marketing course for the health-coaching program developed by renowned pediatrician Dr. Bill Sears and his son, Dr. Jim Sears, co-host of *The Doctors.* Emerson Ecologics, the leading distributor of dietary supplements in the United States, invited me to teach thousands of practitioners how to ignite their success through webinars and workshops, and in their publications. The Nutritional Therapy Association invited me to co-create a new class for them, the Career Development Course, using the PEACE Process as its foundation. I finally launched my first practice-building program, Z School Marketing Mastery, along with my co-creator, Julia Zaslow, earning tens of thousands of dollars on it in just two small launches. Even more important than the money, the program got rave reviews about how it helped holistic practitioners get clarity and make money pursuing their life's calling. Julia and I also co-founded The Prosperous Practitioner Summit to provide guidance from extraordinary practitioners to thousands of healers on how to thrive and realize boundless joy doing their life's work. Natural health companies, organizations, and individuals called to seek my counsel. At last I was finally seeing black versus red on my business balance sheet.

It's painful thinking about the number of people in this world who have struggled and suffered because of our broken disease management system. We must educate our patients, clients, friends, and family to take control of their health and avoid needlessly putting themselves in harm's way. To do this involves building an army of holistic practitioners who can financially weather the ups and downs of the economy and create thriving practices for the long term. We have to stop the "brain drain" from the holistic community before more lives are senselessly destroyed. I know I can do this with your help.

You deserve to achieve your financial goals in a conscious way that's consistent with your values and philosophy of healing. The PEACE Process reflects this approach. I wrote *The PEACE Process* so that if anyone says to you, "You're going to fail," you'll have the confidence to smile and say, "No way! I'm going to *flourish*." It will require some big leaps and learning on your part, but I will show you the path right now, right here.

Introduction

As a holistic health practitioner, you want to help people heal. You want people to lead happier and healthier lives. You want to teach them that there is a better solution than taking "pills for ills" to fix their problems. You want your positive energy to flow into your community.

But you're realistic. You know that to achieve your goals and help others, you need to grow your business. You cannot throw a life preserver to someone caught in the waves unless you're standing on solid ground. Without a firm business platform from which to operate, you'd be flailing about in the current with them. You'd be unable to help.

Your flourishing business is the safe rock from which you can toss a life preserver. A successful career dedicated to healing goes hand in hand with sound business-building practices. In *The PEACE Process* I'll show you how to transform your dreams into something solid and dependable, even thrillingly successful. It's possible!

In the following pages you'll learn how to reconnect to your purpose and build a thriving practice using the proven methods I teach to healers and students throughout the United States. I believe you'll find my ideas liberating. They will remove the barriers and dislodge you from whatever is keeping you from generating the success you want and deserve.

This book was developed specifically for holistic, functional, and integrative health practitioners, students, schools, and clinics. I've seen naturopathic doctors (NDs), medical doctors, acupuncturists, oriental medical doctors (OMDs), chiropractors (DCs,) osteopathic doctors (DOs), nutritionists, herbalists, reiki masters, yoga therapists, massage therapists, energy workers, and health coaches make significant business gains by putting the PEACE Process into play.

If you fit into one of the above categories and are wondering whether or not this book applies to you, the answer is absolutely "Yes!" Regardless of whether you're just getting started or have been at it a while and want to see bigger gains in your bottom line, this book will show you how to build a booming practice using my method—the PEACE Process.

These strategies work regardless of whether you legally call your customer a client or a patient. Throughout this book I use those terms interchangeably, so don't get too hung up on *client* versus *patient*; I'm simply trying to be inclusive.

As you read the following pages, remember this one important fact: promoting your practice is not something you do once and set aside. You will never be able to tick off "marketing" on your to-do list and sit back and wait for the business to roll in. It's a continuous activity, week after week, year after year.

I understand the challenges of your work. If you own or run a practice, you wear multiple hats: chief clinician, chief executive, chief marketing officer. Let up on any one of those roles and you put your practice and your future (and those of your patients!) at grave risk. This book will show you why *now* is the best possible time to kick your practice-building efforts into gear, and will give you the steps to make it happen.

You'll learn a lot in the following pages, but please don't get overwhelmed! Just take things one small step at a time. Each action will take you one bit closer to where you want to go, which is one step more than you might otherwise have taken. Marketing, like any new activity in your life, is a learned behavior. Much like taking on a new diet or exercise regimen, the more you do it the more habitual and comfortable it becomes.

If your occupation or calling is different from that of the holistic practitioner down the street from you, you'll probably get something different out of the PEACE Process than they will. But regardless of where you are, following the ideas in this book will get you closer to your ideal practice, I promise.

If you dread the thought of spending your time and energy on online marketing, social media, public speaking, and website up-dates, take heart. You will soon learn that once you get my marketing methods in place, you'll actually be able to spend time doing the things you truly love more than ever before—like heal *greater numbers of patients* than you are right now.

After all, isn't that what you want?

1. Getting Started

Why do holistic practitioners struggle to survive? Some practitioners blame market conditions, but that doesn't explain why some falter while others thrive even when the economy is bad.

Others claim it's the lack of acceptance of holistic health care by the public, but that argument doesn't cut it anymore. In fact, an analysis of complementary and alternative medicine (CAM) in US medical-school curricula was undertaken in 2015. It was discovered that half of the 130 schools (50.8 percent) offered at least one CAM course or clerkship. A total of 127 different course listings were identified, including traditional medicine, acupuncture, spirituality, and herbs. If so many medical schools are offering courseware to their students, you can bet it's because the public is seeking it!

Still others cite a small market. Yet record numbers of people are using alternative therapies. The demand for holistic and integrative care has never been stronger.

And of course, there are the traditional triple threats that lead to business failure in any profession: mismanagement, marketing missteps, and financial fumbles. They can happen to anybody, if you let them.

Why do holistic practitioners too often fail? I ask this question a lot. And I believe one of the biggest factors behind the failure of holistic businesses is an obstacle that you are fully capable of cutting through. I call it "noise." I'm not discounting the impact of the problems I mentioned above on the failure rate, and I'll certainly be putting those marketing missteps to rest. But assuming you have ruled out mismanagement, marketing missteps, and financial fumbles, what's left is *noise*.

Today's consumer is being blasted with an unprecedented number of health-care remedies, leaving them stuck in a quagmire of options. Which food is the problem: sugar, gluten, dairy, red meat, or soy? When they "search" their condition on the internet (which they do 90 percent of the time they have a problem), how many solutions are they bombarded with? Should they see a doctor, nutritionist, chiropractor, naturopath, acupuncturist, shaman, or health coach? Should they go for the pill, the surgery, the cooking class, or a healing retreat? People are paralyzed. Their inertia traps you, too, right between their indecision and your monthly bills. Cutting through the clutter of all this noise is your best shot to not only help them find relief but find your own path to a financially thriving business. But how do you start?

By getting hard-core about your focus.

The key is to make it super easy for prospective clients to find you amid all the noise. Positioning yourself as an unfocused healer who helps everyone with everything just adds to the confusion your ideal client is already experiencing.

The solution is to reinvent your position in the marketplace. Establish exactly whom you serve and how you can save them. Rise up and plant your flag as the trusted authority and expert who can change lives and give people exactly what they want. Proper positioning is a game-changer and the number-one way to thrive in our culture of distraction and information overload.

The PEACE Process

You can grow your practice without sacrificing a lot of time, energy, or money—and certainly not patient care—in the process. You can comfortably and consciously promote your services to the masses and actually feel good about it! Your path to get there is the PEACE Process.

This method works. I've witnessed its power in my own practice and with other successful holistic leaders. A word of caution, however: It's simple, but it will take a bit of work. Let's face it, there's no easy path to any place worth going.

PEACE is an acronym for five steps: Purpose, Establish, Attract, Connect, and Engage. Each term is summarized below. Before we go there, I'd like to explain why I specifically chose the term *"PEACE"* and not some other acronym instead. Some have asked whether it's because my method is a kinder, gentler approach to this whole business of marketing. Yes, it is, but more important, "The PEACE Process" is an easy-to-remember phrase. If you ever get stuck on what to do next it will be easy to recall "The PEACE Process" and its five steps. And you will gain more confidence and calm just knowing that you have in your hand the how-to guide to success. Still, I primarily chose "The PEACE Process" for a very different—and personal—reason.

On May 4th, 1970, members of the Ohio National Guard fired into a crowd of Kent State University demonstrators, killing four and wounding nine Kent State students. My brother Eric was one of the protestors on that dreadful day in our nation's history. This event was profoundly life-changing for him! Eric was committed to the peace process and was willing to defend his beliefs that day and for many years thereafter. My book is not about endorsing a political ideology; it's about honoring Eric and his passion. Without his tragic story, it's unlikely that my path would have unfolded in the manner in which it did. Naming my method in honor of something that was so central to his life seemed most fitting.

Here are the steps:

Purpose

> When it comes to building a marketing foundation, step one is to tap in to your connection to your purpose, or mission, and know how this connection clears your path toward peak performance. Many marketing books fail because they do not connect marketing success to *your purpose*. They offer plenty of strategies and tactics, but like a boat without a rudder, over time you find yourself all alone out there, blowing around in the open water and not sure exactly what to do or where to go when things don't go quite as planned. Connection to your purpose keeps you moving forward toward your goal even on those days when things feel challenging.

Establish

People seek the expert to help them heal. I'll show you how to promote your services to a specific niche market and establish your position as a trusted authority. Once you take this step, it will be much easier for your audience to find you in a crowded and noisy market.

Attract

No one wants to chase down new clients; you want them to find you instead! I lay out the methods for attracting prospects to your practice in a practical, low-cost, and conscious way. This step explains how to set up compelling marketing messages, both when writing and speaking, that draw people to you. Your online messaging is especially important here. After all, if 90 percent of your prospective clients are going online to look for you, you'd better make sure they a) can find you, and b) will hang around your website long enough to learn how you can help them.

Connect

It is important to understand what motivates prospects to buy your services. You might be surprised to learn that using your web presence as an online advertisement—whether it's your website or social media—is the fastest path toward frustration and failure. People buy from people they know, like, and trust. If you strive to build deep connection with prospective clients instead of constantly promoting yourself and your services, you will be amazed at the change in your business results. *Connection delivers paying clients.*

Engage

If you want to learn the secret to authentically and ethically converting prospective patients or clients into raving fans in a one-to-one setting without feeling uncomfortable or sleazy, you are going to adore this step! Not only will you learn how to pace yourself in a sales situation, but you'll learn how to deal with the "money talk": asking for cash for services, justifying your prices, and all the other difficult conversations about payment that most people hate.

In the following chapters, each of the PEACE steps is explained along with examples, formulas, and templates you can model and use in your practice. Each step of the process builds on the one before it; they are sequential. Once you master these steps, you will continually dash up and down the staircase throughout your practice-building efforts over time... but you must first build the staircase!

To get the most out of this book I encourage you to challenge yourself with my exercises. It's best to read it in a distraction-free zone, take lots of notes, and make sure you're crystal clear on each idea before moving on to the next one. I also encourage you to read the whole book before taking the individual steps to their conclusions. Once you have digested the big picture, following the steps will make much more sense and flow more easily.

Now let's get on with it!

2. Purpose

Okay, I get it: You're not madly in love with the idea of running a business, and especially not keen on marketing your services. You've pretty much told me that you'd rather have root canal surgery than devote time to selling. You know you have to get around this aversion to marketing. But how?

Getting comfortable with marketing starts by connecting to your big purpose—your "why." Visionary thinker Simon Sinek explains this brilliantly in his book *Start with Why*. He says something that's quite revolutionary: People don't buy *what* you do; they buy *why* you do it.

When you connect to your purpose, people are inspired to follow you, to listen to you, to believe in you. To buy from you, too. That's why *purpose* is the first step in my PEACE Process. When you reconnect to your purpose, your passion and vigor show up. You become laser-focused on what's important in your life, which sets the stage for doing the right things in your practice—the things that push you forward and help you deflect the things that keep you stuck. *Things that move the needle.* It's the foundation for all your marketing efforts.

You probably came to this work with the noble cause of healing others, but you might have pushed that purpose aside in the midst of your "busyness." Over time, like any thought or behavior, your lack of mindful, purposeful connection to your "why" becomes flabby, out of shape, and weak. A weak purpose precipitates a sagging practice.

But maybe there's something else going on here. Lots of experts proclaim, "Follow your purpose! Follow your passion!" But what the heck does that mean and why is it so hard to do day after day?

Following your purpose and *deeply integrating with it* are two very different things. I believe that integrating with your "why" requires you to become more selfish. You heard me right: *selfish.* Here's what I mean:

Many years ago in a *Life* magazine interview, Mother Teresa was asked why she did the work she did. She didn't answer, "I want to ease the suffering of the orphaned, the sick, and the poor." She said that she did it because of "the way it makes me feel." Mother Teresa helped the disadvantaged for a more intrinsic, more selfish reason than perhaps you thought. Her self-centered motives were clearly not a bad thing! But the need for her to continue to feel great about helping people was the driver that kept her going, never wavering in her mission.

When I receive an email or feedback after a workshop and someone says, "Wow, thanks so much for putting me on the road to success," of course I'm gratified that someone has found direction in their work. But what I adore every bit as much is the way I feel after the feedback! I'm floating around, grinning like an idiot because positive feedback makes me feel powerful, unstoppable, and proud of my work.

I used to feel ashamed about this. When I was a kid, talking about our achievements was considered bragging and was discouraged. I was taught to fit in, not stand out, and not to brag, because after all, "What would people think?" As a society, we are taught to be humble about our accomplishments and to discuss our successes in a way that demonstrates that we did things for the benefit of others. As a result we've swung this pendulum too far in the opposite direction! Believe me, there are plenty of people out there who should ratchet down their public self-adoration. But there is absolutely, positively nothing wrong with feeling proud and powerful about your achievements.

Embrace your success! When receiving testimonials and praise, there isn't a darn thing wrong with feeling that, yes, you are awesome and you are great at what you do. In fact, I truly believe that you must grab on to that personal power, because when things get rough in your business—and they most certainly will—having these gems in your back pocket will drive you forward through the low periods. Doing good deeds for selfish reasons is perfectly acceptable.

After all, if Mother Teresa was okay with it, you should be, too.

When You Lose Your "Why," You Lose Your Way

When the storms of life hit and the cash isn't coming in fast enough, you start to question what you're doing. You might randomly start doing a million things to try to generate income. This usually delivers pathetic results. I call this activity "breaking branches."

A number of years ago, my husband and I went on vacation to Maui with another couple—let's call them Fred and Wilma. One morning we decided to take a drive up the coast to a place that had great snorkeling. We loaded up the car and drove to this amazing cove. Not wanting to waste a second getting into that clear, beautiful, warm water, we all jumped out of the car at the same time.

The problem was, in our haste to dash to the beach, our friends locked the keys in the car. Since we were in the middle of nowhere with no one else in sight, we were pretty much up a creek. Fred spent the next hour yelling at Wilma (he felt it was her fault, even though he had driven us there), and she started running around looking for objects that she could jam into the window to unlock the door and get the keys, which were sitting in plain view on her seat where Fred had tossed them before jumping out of the car.

Wilma ran over to a hedgerow and began breaking branches off it looking for the exact size and shape that she could shove in through a slight crack in the top of the window and ultimately hook the door lock on a little offshoot of the branch. Branch by branch, she continued her task. After about a half-dozen failed attempts at this, we heard someone yelling in the background. We looked up to find a local gardener running at us sputtering, "Stop that, I just planted them! Those are brand new bushes!"

Wilma was doing what I've seen practitioners do every day in their marketing work. They wait until they're in an emergency situation—their client load has dried up, they panic about how they're going to pay next month's rent—and they go into marketing mayhem, trying out one thing after another (breaking branches) with no real logic, common sense, or method to their madness. In the end, none of the scattershot tactics work, at least not long term. They just end up with a lot of broken branches, damaged hedges, and no keys to unlock the door to success.

You wouldn't sell a client a bunch of random supplements and hope that something works, would you? Of course not. You would follow a system or process to determine what they need and the steps to help them achieve success. Just as in your clinical work, when it comes to marketing your practice there is a method that must be followed in order to ensure the best possible outcome. That method is the PEACE Process. Connecting to your purpose is its first and most important step.

Purpose Destroys Your Three Big Threats

Even with all the best-baked plans, there are three worrisome things that threaten your success as time goes on: distraction, interruption, and limited willpower. They're worrisome because they're hardwired into us.

Distraction

In primitive times, distraction was necessary in order for us to survive. Imagine you're out in the field collecting wild berries and hunting small game for your next meal. There's a baby strapped to your back as you do your work. A lot of things are going on in your environment that you need to be aware of at the same time: You check for movement in the brush around you, making sure there isn't a wild animal looking at you for *his* next meal. You pay attention to the storm clouds collecting in the sky above in case you need to run for cover. Perhaps there's someone from a neighboring tribe who stumbles upon you and might not be so friendly. In this ancient world, being distracted was not only important, it was critical for your very survival. And as you know, survival trumps everything.

Being wired to survive predisposes us to distraction and multi-tasking. Today our fears are less about being hunted by other predators and more about reading email while participating in conference calls and watching webinars while posting to our Facebook pages.

The problem is that although you might think you can do multiple things well at one time, it is a widely dispelled myth that multitasking is effective. In study after study it's been shown that multitasking doesn't just slow you down and increase the number of mistakes you make, it temporarily *changes the way your brain works*. "Splitting the brain" through multitasking slows your progress and kills focus.

We all get distracted while we're working, of course. That's not surprising. But what *is* surprising—and more than a little troubling—is how long it takes the average person to refocus on work *after* losing their train of thought.

A study conducted at the University of California, Irvine, a couple of years ago showed that most people take twenty-three minutes and fifteen seconds to recover from a distraction or interruption. Imagine how just the simple act of refocusing can add up (and steal precious time) over the course of a day!

Interruption

Our inclination (and desire) to be interrupted comes from the latest research in neuroscience. In his book *The Shallows*, author Nicholas Carr explains how our use of electronics is becoming a physical addiction. For example, every time we check our smartphone or any other electronic messaging device, the texts, emails, and posts trigger a release of dopamine into our system. We love the feeling we get from that dopamine "hit"! As a result, we continually check, check, check for messages. Has someone responded to my mail? Has someone "liked" my Facebook post? Has that important person accepted my LinkedIn connection? Our craving isn't just emotional; we can become *physically addicted to the dopamine high*. It was the psychologist B. F. Skinner who demonstrated this idea of "random reinforcement." He had a rat push a lever one hundred times, and every one-hundredth time it was given a piece of food. Skinner discovered that if you offer the reward more randomly, it's even more exciting to the rat. Same for us, only we keep "pushing the lever" on our email or social media applications. We know that most of the time what we'll see is pretty boring, but it's that random excitement (and desire for a dopamine reward) that keeps us checking our messages over and over and over.

I'm increasingly alarmed by the number of people I see walking on the beach, eyes glued to their smartphones, paying no attention to the waves, seabirds, or—even worse—their own loved ones walking beside them (who are, by the way, looking at their smartphones, too). Now I understand the mechanics behind this. Not only are we addicted, it's now commonly believed that we are rewiring the circuitry in our brains through this behavior. We will *need* the high at some point.

This is scary stuff.

Limited Willpower

Some of the research I've seen about willpower from Dr. Roy Baumeister and his colleagues explains much about why so many of us have difficulty with focus throughout the day. In their studies over the past ten years, they've concluded that willpower is like a muscle. It can become fatigued with use, and cannot perform indefinitely.

Say you're working on a very taxing project or task—maybe you're creating a new program in your practice, doing some research, or writing your book. Have you noticed that after a few hours of mentally challenging work you find yourself unable to think anymore? That you've basically run out of steam? There's a reason for that. Willpower works a lot like muscle glycogen. As you know, the body has a limited reserve of muscle glycogen that gets depleted after a bout of intense exercise, and to continue your physical effort you must replenish your glycogen stores by consuming food. With willpower, it's your mental energy that's limited; you have only a certain amount stored up to complete difficult tasks. Once you've tapped out your willpower reserves, you're unable to make smart decisions and feel you can't go on. In fact, continuing in a productive manner is often impossible. When you "hit the wall," you should take a break and replenish your "willpower glycogen." Unfortunately, if you're like most people, you simply power through to complete your task.

I've personally experienced this in action. I used to work out of a home office that had a sliding glass door leading out onto a small patio. Sitting on this patio was a potted ficus tree that despite my long history of murdering household foliage was growing out of control—so much so that its leafy branches were literally blocking all the sunlight that came into my office. This drove me crazy! The room was already dimly lit, and that overgrown ficus made it even worse. But like so many things in life, I tolerated it day after day.

One morning I'd been working hard on a big project and found myself squinting to read some research articles to back up my hypothesis. I was feeling distracted and restless, and that ficus tree became the object of my irritation. I finally decided to go outside and give that tree a haircut. Fifteen minutes later, with nearly an entire forest eradicated, I walked back into my brightly lit office loaded with energy and focus! I honestly couldn't believe how taking a break (and taking care of an annoyance to boot) completely recharged my willpower.

Pushing on to complete a tough task while weary often results in exhaustion and lackluster results. This third threat is such a sneaky one that you might not even realize just how badly it's blocking your progress.

These three big threats add to the feeling of being stuck. There are plenty of tactics you can put into play to counter these problems, but unless you first anchor yourself to your big purpose and tap in to it, not much else matters.

Getting "purpose fit" doesn't work 100 percent of the time, but it works better than anything else I've seen or done in my life. When I find myself off track for any reason, the little framed photo I have on my desk of me and my big brother is all it takes for me to buckle down and do something, anything, even one small thing, toward making progress. Eric's story is what helps me dislodge from inertia and get my momentum back.

Your written purpose manifesto, explained further on, can do the same for you. The more you tell your story, write about it, feel the feelings all over again, and nurture the connection you have to it, the stronger your will to push through the myriad of things that fight for your attention.

How Can You Change the World If You Can't Pay Your Rent?

All too often I find myself talking with a holistic practitioner who feels uncomfortable about the idea of promoting themselves or their services. It's as if marketing and sales are somehow at odds with fulfilling their life's purpose.

Chances are you're not independently wealthy—only a tiny fraction of the population can actually claim that. I'm guessing you're not a nonprofit operation either. In fact, if you wanted to do charity work, you'd probably do something a whole lot different from (and a whole lot easier than!) what you're doing now. This is your profession, every bit as important as the schoolteacher, the autoworker, and the manager at the bank. But unlike those who work for other people, you're an entrepreneur. In order to financially thrive—to place yourself upon that rock from which you can throw the drowning person a life preserver—you must position your value to others and promote your services to your market.

If you believe with all your heart that your work can change people's lives, then any negativity surrounding the idea of self-promotion must be put aside. In fact, if you have the ability to change the course of someone's fate, to *not* promote your solution is tantamount to extreme neglect. People not only need but want your help, and they're more than willing to pay for it. For the good of your community, your fear, uncertainty, doubt, or loathing regarding sales and marketing must be eliminated, just like you tell your patients to eliminate toxic foods or unhealthy habits. Practice development is an essential business skill, and like all business skills, if you don't learn it you'll go broke... *fast*.

Perhaps even more important is how you will feel at the end of your life if you do not accomplish your dreams of healing people; if you have to work for somebody else in order to pay the rent; if the only thing standing in your way is some mental programming that came from who-knows-where that selling is bad, wrong, hard, or unethical.

The world needs you and your gifts. Don't let *anything* block your path to delivering them.

Create Your Visceral Trigger to Battle Your Demons

You will be tested. You will have your moments of fear, uncertainty, and doubt. And you will have naysayers. Oh boy, will you ever.

When I feel that "failure tape" playing in my head—which typically shows up in the middle of the night—it's my purpose that kicks things back into gear. I have literally rewired my brain to snap out of the negativity the instant I feel that sinking feeling in the pit of my stomach. I do it by calling up a certain memory—a visceral, powerful reminder of why I'm taking on this important work.

The memory I use is this: I'm looking at my brother's casket lying in the bottom of a dreadfully dark hole in the ground. Sadness is suffocating me. I toss a rose onto the top of his casket and look over to Eric's sixteen-year-old son, face frozen, emotionless, in shock. I hear my mother's wails and see the anger in her eyes. I watch her as she stumbles next to my dad, grabbing his hand as she collapses in a miserable heap of tears and grief. I can actually feel my heart break in that moment.

By the end of this visualization exercise I'm pretty much ready to kick ass and take names, including those of the naysayers in (and now out of) my life. I know that to *not* move forward is a betrayal of Eric, my mom, and all those people out there who have faced the same fate or worse. In fact, I can't *not* move forward. I must be able to look back at my life in my golden years and say, "Yes, I did that. I made a difference. I changed the course of people's lives!" That visceral trigger keeps me focused and sane, and calling up yours will help you during those low times, too.

Exercise: Get Purpose Fit

To get "purpose fit," this exercise will strengthen your resolve.

Write your answers to the following questions, and once completed, develop a one-page purpose statement that you emotionally connect to. When you—or anyone else—reads this statement, it should tug at the heart, activate the gut, or maybe even arouse anger or frustration. *Feeling something* is key—it's this pull that not only keeps your head in the game but attracts people to you, especially people who align with you and want to work with you. Without that tug it becomes yet another meaningless, bland mission statement that gets buried in a business plan or parked on your website, soon to be forgotten and relegated to the land of ho-hum.

Here are the questions:

- What made you choose your health profession?
- What condition or health issue makes you so mad that it brings you close to tears?
- What story compelled you to change the course of your life?

- What health issues have you or someone close to you struggled with?
- What or who in life inspired you and your work, and why?
- When growing up, what did you love to do more than anything else?
- How did you feel when you decided to take on this work?
- Imagine you're at the end of your career, and ask yourself, "What important work did I do? Whom did I help? What am I most proud of?"
- What professional accomplishments must occur in order for you to consider your career satisfying—one with few or no regrets?

Once you've answered these questions, compile a manifesto—any page-length will do—that integrates your thoughts. There is no template to follow on this; it should be the kind of essay that a stranger could pick up and read and understand exactly who you are today and the dreams and accomplishments you hope to achieve in the future. Your goal isn't to make it as concise as possible, but to pour your heart into it. You might even cry a little as you write. That's a good thing—it means you hit a nerve and connected to something big. When you feel stuck, take a break for several hours before reviewing and revising what you wrote. Distance will bring clarity; your breaks are an essential part of the process.

When you feel you're done with your essay, read it over every morning until it becomes a part of you, like an organ. Not your appendix, which can be removed, silly—an organ like your heart.

This step is a life-changer. It will help you reengage with your passion and plant the seeds of focus and fortune. Believe me; it changed mine and those of many others with whom I've worked.

3. Establish

No one can be all things to all people *and* be effective. That's crazy. And not only that, if this sounds like the kind of practice model you aspire to create, you're risking your ability to become an expert at any one thing and make a significant impact on the health of your community. Perhaps my next story will sound familiar to you.

When I finished my nutrition studies in 2006, I wanted to help everyone with every health challenge on the planet. I signed up for every health conference, studied every disease and condition, and learned about as many supplements and their therapeutic value as I could. I devoured every book that crossed my path on anything having to do with nutritional therapy. I ran myself ragged just trying to stay on top of all the new literature that was coming out about holistic health. I didn't realize it at the time, but I was racing down the fast track to exhaustion and failure.

The only way out of this madness is to target a specific niche market to work with. I can hear the worry in your voice as you say,

"But I don't want to limit myself. I want to help everyone!" But casting your net out as far and wide as possible is the exact opposite of what has proven to be the path to success for all kinds of businesses, including yours.

Unless you pick a ridiculously tiny market—like thirty-two-year-old men who are fifteen pounds overweight, balding, and want to get rid of foot fungus—you'll have all the business you can handle. The population you target will be huge, and so will your revenue opportunities, especially if you offer your services in ways other than one-on-one in-office consultations (be sure to read the chapter called "Advanced Step: Your Signature Platform" later in the book). *Narrowing down* your marketing focus leads to *increased* financial and clinical results. And besides, if that poor balding young man does show up for help, you can certainly help him! The niche market you select and the person you work with might not always be one and the same; indeed, niching is about whom you *seek*, not whom you *serve*. Identifying a niche is about focusing your time, energy, and money toward establishing your place in the market and being discovered by a desperate community that is looking for your support.

A fear that many practitioners have about niching involves the very essence of—and distinction in—the way holistic and functional healers practice compared to our compadres in the allopathic community. In other words, we don't "deconstruct" the human condition or isolate solutions for "broken" or poorly functioning body systems in piecemeal fashion; we consider the whole being, including the various epigenetic or individual biochemical factors—and more—that might be at play. Remember that *how* you work and *whom* you work with are two distinct things! The way you sleuth out the problem—to get to root cause and support optimal function—is consistent with your standard holistic or functional methodology regardless of whether a person comes in with mood issues or itchy skin.

One more question that may be in your mind is whether there is enough room for you in the niche you would like to serve. Can you truly offer something unique if others also choose to work with your same target clients? This concern is a double-edged sword; there are many people who need help and not enough holistic practitioners to serve them. As long as you live in an area with a reasonably sized population and you select a niche that isn't extremely rare or tiny, there will be plenty of clients to go around regardless of how many others focus on that same niche. In fact, this is exactly where the strength of niching shows up. When everyone chooses a general or "I help everyone with everything" strategy, the competition becomes massive, and clients decide who to work with based on who has the lowest fees. (And trust me, the fastest way to fail is to race to the bottom through discounting.) But by diversifying, holistic healers within a geographic area become a powerful referral network in which everyone wins. I dream of the day when holistic practitioners collaborate instead of compete when it comes to serving communities with natural health therapies. This is best accomplished through niching.

Do people seek health care when they're feeling great? Rarely. And few, if any, look for a practitioner for wellness or healthy aging. Even in the conventional world, the main reason people go to a family doctor for annual checkups is to get lab tests done to make sure they aren't showing signs of disease, not for health promotion. They want help when they have a pain, problem, or condition that is going unresolved. They've had it. When they're finally ready for help, they want something very specific: a specialist, not a generalist. They don't type "general practitioner who does everything for everyone" into their online search engine. In fact, they're looking for the exact opposite. They seek a solution that is personal and delivers a customized outcome that will fix their specific problems or fulfill their unique needs once and for all.

Let's look at a scenario that one of your prospective patients could be facing. Ernie has just been told by his family doctor that he has blockage in two of his coronary arteries along with elevated inflammatory markers. Since he lost his dad and brother to heart attacks, Ernie worries that if he doesn't start making changes in his life, he, too, might meet an early demise.

He has a zillion questions in his head: What should he eat? What shouldn't he eat? What sort of activity might help him? Can too much exercise make things worse? What about specific supplements—will anything help? What can he expect from taking pharmaceutical drugs, and is there any way can he avoid taking them completely? Can he still have sex or is there a chance he'll drop dead in the middle of a moment of passion? At what point will a catheterization be necessary, or can he avoid surgery altogether?

Now, to whom do you think Ernie will go for help—back to his one-size-fits-all general practitioner? Not if he has any brains! He will seek out an authority in the area of heart disease. And if Ernie's inclined to seek holistic or functional medicine first (again, a wise man would), he will seek out a health-care practitioner who specializes in heart health—one with vast experience and a proven record working with and helping people who are struggling with exactly the same condition he has. Wouldn't you?

The world is rife with examples of companies that have come to the brink of collapse simply by not getting—or staying—focused on a tight niche market with specific needs. Whether it's the infamous story of Sears department stores and its misguided foray into real estate and blue chip stocks, or the financial struggles of daily newspapers trying to share all the news with everyone, the fact remains that if you do not target a specific audience with a precise solution, you might as well be invisible when it comes to being discovered in a crowded, noisy market. Being all things to all people is a formula for failure.

By the way, if you're going to use the argument that general practitioners are all things to everyone, so why can't *you* be... I invite you to explore how GPs are faring these days. They spend less time than ever before with patients and are leaving their profession in record numbers due to burnout, stress, and financial strain.

Marketing authorities have written volumes about niching, and all of it comes down to one basic fact: You have to focus on a specific slice of the market to build a thriving business. This applies to all sizes and types of health practices, including yours.

I can guarantee that if you refuse to narrow your scope, you risk being invisible to those seeking your services, and your bottom line will suffer, too.

A New Definition of Niche

You probably think of a niche as a demographic, such as "middle-aged women who are going through menopause." But that's just one piece of the puzzle; in fact, that is a target audience rather than a niche. I define niche differently. I view niching as providing a unique and specialized solution that delivers a desired outcome to your target population's unmet desire. That's a lot of stuff in there, right? But here it is again, boiled down into a more digestible formula:

I help [target audience] to [accomplish what] so they can [outcome they want].

We'll come back to this statement a little later. For now I want to plant the idea and expand your thinking to include a more comprehensive picture of what the term *niche* means.

Your niche is "organic" in nature, meaning it:

- **Is flexible and evolving.** As you identify a specific niche around which to fashion your marketing, keep an open mind to new ideas, therapies, and related markets that would allow you to modify your definition. Don't try to get this perfect! Allow some room for adjustment. Trust me. The specifics *will* change over time.

- **Delivers outcomes that people want.** Keep in mind that the outcome your clients seek isn't a "program" or a particular certification of yours; they want resolution for their issues. Your method to get them there, in other words *how* you deliver your services (such as nutrition counseling, acupuncture, mindfulness, food sensitivity testing), is less important to them than the results they'll get from working with you.

- **Speaks to your heart, your talent, your mission.** Create your niche and your programs with your clients in mind. That said, if you aren't *intrinsically motivated* by the services you provide and the people you work with, your practice will not have staying power.

- **Is unique and special; it sets you up to be the market leader in that specialty.** Differentiation is foundational for client attraction. Your niche must be unique enough to rise above the fray, yet not too "out there" so as to minimize your market opportunity.

Earlier I wrote that a niche is not simply a demographic but rather is about providing a unique and specialized solution that delivers an outcome that this demographic desires. Perhaps you will address a health condition that a specific population struggles with. But that's just one possible way to niche. Another way to think about niching is to consider people in a particular circumstance, or who share a common set of concerns, beliefs, or desires. Examples of this are:

- Busy moms who need fast, healthy recipes for their families
- Athletes who want to build lean muscle and endurance
- Aging women who want to feel and look younger
- Young couples who want help to conceive
- Individuals who worry about getting a specific condition because it "runs in the family"

As you will see in the next chapter, "Attract," the primary objective of niching is to simplify and inform your marketing outreach (with the added benefit of making you an authority). That's because understanding your niche market's deep desires allows you to position your services to prospects with laser-like clarity in an increasingly busy and largely generic market, making it significantly easier for them to find you among the masses of options.

Over time your interests will change, and new information and ideas will provide opportunities to revise your niche. Don't worry that once you define your niche you cannot ever change it or broaden it. Not so! If you're in business, your goal is to always be open to new possibilities and shift your focus accordingly. But regardless of how you shift, targeting your services—or at least a portion of them—toward a specific population will always be necessary in order to be discovered by new prospective clients.

What Outcome Do People Want from You, Anyway?

The real value of niching is understanding what your ideal client truly desires and demonstrating how your service can perfectly fulfill that desire. What transformation do clients want to experience as a result of working with you? Understanding this is the secret sauce when it comes to attracting new clients (pardon the fast-food reference). Most people are used to using insurance to pay for their healthcare costs. If you run a direct-pay business, they are choosing to invest in you instead of that weekend getaway or new dress. It's a big step for many people—a real leap of faith. So it has to be worth it to them!

Articulating how your services will help them get exactly what they want is very important. In fact, if you take nothing else away from this book, knowing how to match your services to your clients' desires can change your fortunes. It's that big.

So let's consider the niche formula one more time: I help [target audience] to [accomplish what] so they can [outcome they experience].

I want you to devote attention to the outcome, the "so they can" part of this statement. This piece of the niche formula is often overlooked or missed completely. Here's why it's important: The average person is rarely emotionally driven to lower their cholesterol level or lose fifty pounds. They might seem *excited* by such improvements, but if you peel back the layers what you'll find is that losing fifty pounds is likely about looking hot in their skinny jeans, fitting into a plane seat without the embarrassment of a seat-belt extender, living longer so they can see their grandkids go off to college, turning heads at their class reunion—you catch my drift? It's the emotional connection to the desired outcome—not a lab number—that drives behavior. That's why it's important to get that outcome piece of the formula nailed down.

Setting up your service offerings without first understanding what your niche truly wants is backwards. It's far more powerful to develop your solution with the end in mind. Not with the end that you want, but with the unmet needs, wants, and desires of your niche market—essentially the outcome *they* want to achieve. And what do they want? Here's a clue: It's not you, your services, or a laundry list of your credentials. Not at first, anyway. They want something that's much more specific and personal to them.

There's never been a better time or easier path to find out what your ideal client wants from you. Here are my top three ways to research these things:

Google Alerts

The first research method is through Google Alerts (GA). This tool lets you stay current on what's happening on the web (sans social media) regarding your niche market. You *will* need to set up a Google account to use this handy tool; simply search "Google Alerts" for setup instructions.

First decide what you want Google to track for you, and what you're hoping to achieve. Your goals might include:

- Watching for positive (or negative) mentions of your business or personal name and brand so you can react quickly
- Seeing what major blogs and news sites say about your niche, your competitors, or your special area of interest so you can stay on top of changes and trends
- Finding new blogs and publications that you might be able to contribute content to
- Identifying articles to use in your social media posts

The key benefit of using GA is that it allows you to track your niche-related or business-related keywords or simple phrases within the sources that Google tracks. That means anytime Google sees your keywords and phrases in blogs, forums, news sites, and the wider web, GA will send every mention of one of them (with a link) to you at the frequency you choose. It also tracks mentions on YouTube because as of this writing Google owns that platform.

You will want to set up GA keywords that people in your niche market would use to research their issues. For example, if you're working with women who are going through menopause, you can simply go to Google Alerts and type in terms that the average woman going through menopause might type into a search box. She might type in "symptoms of menopause," "low libido," "hot flashes"—that sort of thing. You can then set up a GA to send you a consolidated email with anything it picks up with those keywords at the frequency you choose.

When you get one of these mail alerts from Google, just scan through the list and click on any link that seems pertinent or otherwise interesting. Use this info to discover what people in your niche market are talking about. What do they want? What are they doing right now to take care of their issue? What is not working for them? You can set up as many of these alerts as you wish. Since Google is the gorilla on the web right now, they're cataloging the bulk of the content being published, so you can feel somewhat confident that Google Alerts is presenting you with the most useful results against your keywords.

Here's a critical point: *Search for phrases that your ideal clients might use.* In other words, don't type in medical terms, technical words, or language that wouldn't necessarily be part of the average person's vocabulary. "Fight free radicals" isn't likely a phrase that your ideal clients will search for; that's language *you* use. They're searching for common, everyday problems in everyday conversation, and their terms are often emotional, personal, basic, and represent the pain and/or desire they have. They're more likely to search for "how to look younger" or "get rid of wrinkles"—the *result* of fighting free radicals; the outcome they're seeking.

Google Alerts is also a great way to see what potential competitors are doing in your niche market. You can conduct a competitive analysis and gain insight into other programs and pricing structures being offered to your niche market. Play around with this a bit just to see what pops up. One huge caveat, though: The more alerts you set up, the more emails you'll receive. You can chew up a lot of time just clicking on all the links you get in these consolidated emails. Once you feel you've found the sweet spot in your keywords, you can cancel out any alerts that aren't delivering valuable links.

One final recommendation: Be sure to set up a Google Alert with your name, your clinic's name, and anything else related to you and your work. That way you'll immediately be notified if someone is using your name on the web—good, bad, or otherwise. Assuming Google picks it up, of course.

LinkedIn Groups

The second way to understand what your niche market wants from you is to use LinkedIn Groups. First, make sure you have your professional LinkedIn page set up as completely as possible. Next, type in whatever keyword, interest, or condition is related to your niche in the search box at the top and click the search button. I usually type in the word "group" next to my search term, too. Play around with multiple terms and ways to express them. For example, for digestive conditions you might search under "gut health groups," "acid reflux groups," "celiac groups," "food sensitivities groups," or "gluten-free groups." Keep trying different terms, as they will each pick up different groups.

As you scour the pages of groups related to those terms, decide which ones you might be interested in joining. You'll want to look at the size of the group and visit the actual group page (if you can) and browse the conversations taking place. You're looking for groups that reflect your ideal patient or client. When you find one you like, ask to join it. By joining these groups you'll be able to "listen in" to the conversation that's going on, what people are struggling with, what they want, what they have tried that works, and what they have tried that doesn't work. Jot down what you find, keep a list of what you're hearing, and especially listen to the *emotional issues* that people are expressing.

Caution: Do *not* start selling your services in these groups! You're merely getting in on the conversation so you can better understand what your ideal client deeply wants. Your initial participation in these groups, if you want to participate at all, is to offer helpful advice and educate. If people love what you post, they'll check you out, I promise. The fastest way to make people disconnect or mistrust you is to start selling your services or asking them to visit your website. Resist the urge to do this. A bit later on you'll learn why "premature promotion syndrome" can crush your chances of success on social media, and how and when to promote yourself effectively and consciously.

By the way, when you create your LinkedIn profile, make sure it is thorough, professional, and engaging. Please use a professional photo, and not that fuzzy shot of you hanging out in the backyard drinking a beer at the family BBQ. Just do a search online or on YouTube for instructions on how to set up a high-quality LinkedIn profile.

Talk to Your Current Clients

The third and best way to learn what your prospective clients want from you is to find out what your current clients are experiencing from working with you. You can glean this knowledge by asking them how your work has transformed them—questions like "What activities are you able to do now that you couldn't do before you came to me?" and "How has working with me changed your outlook on the future of your health?" You are looking for terms that are emotional, powerful, and demonstrate a major shift in their quality of life. Take good notes on what you hear.

Your clients are rarely asked these questions, and the answers offer many benefits to you both. First, you will gain their perspective on things. Instead of measuring your success by seeing lab numbers go from bad to good, you'll get to a deeper level of how your work has made a personal impact on their life, which is the truest measure of success. You'll also establish greater connection with your client, demonstrating that you care about what's going on in their heart and not just on their lab report. This connection is the foundation of loyalty and trust, paramount to long-term clinical and practice success. Finally, you'll discover that all-important aspect of the outcome of your work. The phrases, terms, and emotions that you hear are instrumental in how you position yourself in the marketplace. When it comes to marketing your services, the most powerful messages incorporate terms that your clients use. You'll learn a lot more about this in the upcoming chapter, so stay tuned.

Examples of Niche Statements

Below are some examples from some of the students and practitioners who have attended my workshops. Note how the outcome element in boldface has that emotional quality and more powerfully gets to the heart of what the target population desires:

I help people suffering from joint pain gain freedom from their misery and frustration so they can **enjoy the activities they love once more.**

I help middle-aged women going through menopause manage mood swings and sleep issues so they can **return to a life of endless energy and joy.**

I help busy professional women who agonize over fitting into their favorite pair of jeans lose the muffin-top so they can **feel confident and beautiful.**

I help pregnant women nourish themselves so they can **feel confidant for labor and support post-partum healing.**

I empower children who are distracted and disruptive in the classroom to find better focus so they can **have fun being young (and be fun to be around, too).**

I help people who are concerned about getting a disease because it "runs in the family" take control of their health so they can **feel empowered, beat the odds, and live radiantly.**

Notice in this last statement how the idea of niche is less about a demographic and more about a mindset—a fear or desire. This is a very real population, isn't it? I wanted to share this example so you can broaden the idea of *population* or *audience* to be a group of people who have a similar health concern.

You might be inclined to focus on a population that seeks "health" or "wellness," but that would be a mistake. People seek *solutions* for pain or dysfunction, have a fear or desire, or have something going on that is not resolving. This stems from biology, by the way. Our most basic human instinct is to survive. When things go wrong and we sense that our survival is threatened, the alarms go off, the lights start flashing, and we rush to seek any means possible to reach optimal functioning. But if all is going well, we have no interest in going to a practitioner—we simply aren't wired that way.

Wellness is something you offer—but it's *rarely* what people seek.

Exercise: Pick Your Niche

Let's figure out your niche. Here are some ideas to get your brain wrapped around this. Write down your answers to the following questions:

1. What is your passion or health mission? Are you currently on a journey toward healing from a personal illness? Perhaps you've witnessed a tragedy such as the one in my life that has affected a family member or friend?

2. What health issues are people currently asking for your help with? When you socialize, what do your friends always want to know about? And what do you love helping them with?

3. Who do you know who needs your skills and knowledge the most? What angers you when you look around? Is it childhood obesity? How about the brain-gluten connection? What health issue makes you sad, or so mad that it brings you to tears?

4. What things do you believe you do, have, or know better than nearly everyone you know? What do you love helping other people figure out as it relates to health?

5. Who do you like to hang out with? You're going to spend a lot of time around your clients; make sure that serving this group not only helps them but nurtures you and feeds your soul.

Now think through the population(s) you have identified from the above answers, what issue they want to fix, and what outcome they'll get once it's resolved. For example, if a young mother wants to help her kids better deal with issues of excessive energy or lack of focus, what desired outcome will that bring about for her? Better grades in school? More friends? Less stress in the family? Keep asking the question "What will fixing this issue do for my ideal client?" to get to that answer.

A client of mine was having a hard time coming up with her niche. When I asked her the questions above, she told me that she wanted to help people who were struggling with pain, weight management, blood sugar, and autoimmunity, and who wanted a "life transformation." I knew that with this lack of focus she was going to have a difficult time attracting clients who were seeking a specific outcome. So I asked her to describe this individual in detail; what were the gender, age, lifestyle, frustrations, and fears of this person? Where did this person live, what was their environment like, and what did they want out of life? At the end of the day, if this person had a *great* day, how would they describe it? When my client began to describe her ideal client—her avatar—everything clicked! The breakthrough was that she wanted to help stressed-out moms with teenaged kids who were struggling through the trials and tribulations of their teenage years: kids who did not fit in, were pushing to the point of pain to achieve big things, were not eating right, and so forth. My client realized that it was the stress of taking care of these kids that was *causing* weight gain, physical and emotional pain, and immune system problems for these moms. She now knew her niche and the outcomes her niche wanted and could now pull together everything else—her website, her services and programs, and her messaging.

It's time to develop your niche statement using the template. Write up a few of them and don't try to narrow it down to one just yet. Getting it exactly right is not the goal in this step. Simply play around with it and let it sink in. In time it will become clear. The key is to just get something down on paper and start to noodle on it.

Finally, look at what you've written down and think about it as it relates to your purpose. Is there some synchronicity? People who align their work with their fundamental "why" or core beliefs improve their chance for success. When it comes to your niche statement, you want to make sure that what you're crafting has an emotional tug or pull when you look at it. That's the magic bullet when it comes to staying-power in your practice.

And that's why *purpose* is step one in the PEACE Process.

How to Use Your Niche Formula

The purpose of developing your formula is this: If you're not crystal clear about whom it is you wish to serve, how will you know when your ideal client crosses your threshold? Maybe even more important, how will they know you're right for them?

Burning your formula into your brain gives you the words to say, the content to write, the services to build, and your position in the market when people ask you, "So what do you do?" The goal of creating your formula isn't to write or say it anywhere verbatim, although you can definitely turn your statement into a simple elevator pitch; it's more about knowing who you wish to serve and having the right words on the tip of your tongue to describe the outcome people get when they work with you.

Won't it feel great to know exactly what to say when you introduce yourself to a stranger? When people ask what you do, if you simply say, "I'm a holistic nutritionist," they might ask for more info... then again, maybe not. Giving a job title or professional credential as an introduction typically stops the conversation dead in its tracks.

But if you answer that you help a specific type of person with a focused problem achieve amazing, transformational results, you pull them into your conversation with something they can imagine, something emotional and real to them. You expand the dialog and open the door to possible business. You get more responses like this: "Wow, tell me more! I know someone who could use your help; matter of fact, *I* need your help."

And that's what you want people to say, isn't it?

4. Attract

Now that you know your purpose, who you want to work with, and what outcome you're going to deliver, your next task is to attract your ideal clients to you.

The primary objective in this step of the PEACE Process is to build your list of prospects and clients. This list is your number-one business asset and is essential for driving revenues from your services, programs, and/or special offers. You build your list of clients through the creation and use of powerful marketing messages.

It's said that the average person gets bombarded by over 5,000 marketing messages every day! We're exposed to brands and ads online and off, whether we're surfing the net, streaming videos, listening to tunes on the radio, perusing billboards on the side of the road, or just chatting with a neighbor sporting a polo shirt with his company logo on the pocket. Focused marketing language is critical in order to rise above the noise and be found by your niche market. The way you describe how you help others in your blog, articles, website, social media, videos, public talks, and advertisements—anywhere you put yourself out there to attract new business—is what is known as *messaging*. The impact your message has in the market relies on a number of factors, but most important is how well you connect the dots between what your niche market wants and how your offerings effectively fulfill them.

Messaging Gone Wrong

Why might you need to consider a messaging makeover? The best way to explain this is through a story.

At the turn of the twentieth century, my grandfather, Sam, came to the United States from Eastern Europe with a dream to open a small produce market. Sam and my grandma, Rose, loved food! Sam was an amazing cook (although I must admit his lung stew wasn't one of my favorite dishes). He was passionate about sharing his love of food through selling fresh fruits and veggies to his local community. Sam eventually converted the market into a restaurant; my father managed it and was one of the cooks. My brother Eric set up a restaurant later on, and my brother Marc was a cook on a navy aircraft carrier. My mom was the epitome of an Italian mother, fussing over home-cooked meals at which second helpings were encouraged and gleefully consumed. I had a restaurant many years ago, too, in Boulder, Colorado. Our passion for food has deep roots, to say the least.

Every day Sam would drive two hours from Steubenville, Ohio, to Pittsburgh, Pennsylvania, to pick up his fresh produce at the Strip District on the waterfront and drive two hours back to his market in Steubenville. He'd leave at three in the morning in his twenties-era pickup truck to load up crates and flats of fruits and veggies. Back at his market he'd pick through everything to get them ready for sale.

Sam took an interesting approach to his business. He vehemently refused to sell any piece of fruit with a bruise on it and was known to examine each and every strawberry he purchased and toss out anything that wasn't perfect. Then he'd repackage his blemish-free berries in little cardboard containers and display them for sale.

Here's the rub: Sam refused to price his produce any higher than what his competitors charged; he never compensated for all the "waste" he had paid for. He sold the best product in town at the lowest price. This was a losing financial strategy, of course. Sam eventually went broke and abandoned his dream.

But here's the thing: He could have made it work! My grandpa could have continued with his true calling had he done a better job of positioning his produce market. He could have sent this clear message to his customers: "I've hand-picked every single piece of fruit, and when you buy my strawberries each is going to be perfect—guaranteed. You won't have to throw anything out because I already did it for you. When you see the value I deliver, you'll be happy to pay a little bit more for the very best quality."

Unfortunately I often see this problem in the holistic health industry; we want to be all things to everyone. Offering the best service at the lowest price is neither wise nor possible, and it's the surest path to losing your shirt. Had Sam done a more effective job of messaging, I believe people would have bought those strawberries at a higher price. Message clarity could have saved my granddad's produce market. And it can save you.

The Old Ways of Marketing Are Dead—R.I.P.

Here's the best part about crafting impactful client-attraction messages in today's world: It's never been easier or cheaper.

In the old days, you'd buy an ad in your community magazine or newspaper and hope for the best. You would broadcast a generic message to a mass audience that essentially said, "Come and see me. I'm terrific at what I do. I have these credentials and offer these services. I'm here locally and I'm ready to serve you." The goal was to reach as many people as possible in hopes of attracting new clients, and it was largely thought (and taught) that the best way to do that was to invest big bucks in a broad-based advertising campaign. Prior to the internet, few small businesses had the ability to perform targeted market research, let alone pay for professional services to create custom marketing messages. So the objective was to blast ads out to the multitudes and trust that enough people would see your message and show up.

But this approach doesn't work in today's environment... nor is it necessary. Cutting through the information overload requires more targeted and personalized promotional messages that reach your ideal audience. It involves appealing to the true desires of your niche market. Not only that, but studies now show that people *respond* better to messages that are targeted, show warmth, and feel personal. It's lucky that researching what your niche market wants as I described earlier is pretty much free. Obviously there are some costs associated with putting your web presence together and getting your message out, but attracting patients is significantly more time- and cost-effective than it used to be. There's absolutely no reason why you can't reach exactly whom you want to with the right message without spending an arm and a leg.

Successful practitioners who've been at it a while have also discovered that one of the best ways to attract new prospects through powerful messaging is to listen to the language their current clients are using. What do they want from their clinician? What have they not received from anybody else? How has working with their practitioner transformed them? What can they now do that they were unable to do before? Practitioners have learned to attract new patients by using the exact words and expressed feelings that their current patients use.

These days it's become quite simple to learn what your ideal patient or client wants and then create your marketing messages to reflect those things.

Why Are New Marketing Messages So Important?

There are three reasons. First of all, your prospects can't find you otherwise. If you're not on the first few pages of results when somebody's searching for holistic health services online (which they do most of the time), you'll never get discovered unless they already know your name and are looking for you that way. But they don't. Most of the time a person is simply looking for a practitioner in the local area who specializes in what they want. If you don't hit the top of that search engine listing, you'll never be found. I describe search engine optimization (SEO) in more detail later in the book, but one element of ranking high in search engines is the use of relevant semantic or conversational phrases (read: marketing messages) throughout your online presence. Have you done a web search on yourself lately using terms *other than your name*? Are you showing up anywhere in the first handful of pages? Of course there are no guarantees on anything when it comes to ranking given the crazy complexity of search engine algorithms, but I can say with certainty that without solid messaging your shot of hitting the first few pages is dismal.

Second, people buy what they want from an emotional—not a logical—place. They look for help based on an outcome they seek for a specific desire or problem. So if your marketing messages focus on services and credentials—logical things—but your prospects are only looking for an outcome that has its roots in emotion, such as freedom from pain and misery, the connection won't happen.

I want to dive deep into this idea of emotional messaging, because it often feels counterintuitive. That's because we are used to communicating logically. As children we were taught to speak and write in a proper manner, and to articulate information based on logic, facts, structure, and common sense. Proper sentence structure and good grammar were consistently emphasized and paid off in the way of good grades on homework assignments and projects. In fact, for me the only exception to this focus on logic was a course from my college days called "Oral Interpretation." We were instructed to take a piece of literature, anything at all—no rules!—and present it to the class in speech form using our own tone, voice, humor, character, and, above all else, *emotion*. The goal of the assignment was to move the class; to make the other students feel something inside and not simply hear the words we were saying.

Something amazing happened in that classroom that year. Students who normally followed the rules, who soberly listened to (or maybe slept through) those fifty-three-minute classes, *came alive.* Our presentations lasted no more than five minutes or so, and the variety of works that people dug up to recite blew me away. For my talk I used the story that appeared on the inside jacket of The Who's *Quadrophenia* album cover (remember albums?) because of the emotion it evoked in me when I first read it. The class was fun and we formed a bond—an emotional connection—with one another like you wouldn't believe. In fact, one of my classmates ultimately became my first husband—talk about a convincing oratory! But that, of course, is a story for a different book altogether.

The point I'm making here is this: Emotions attract and connect. They compel us to align with a cause. They incite us to take action. They draw us into relationships. Falling in love is emotional. We buy things emotionally and then justify the purchase later on through reason. If you don't believe me, look around your own home while you think about what you need to survive compared to what you own. Do you really need all those shoes? How about all those holiday decorations? What about the piles of tools, or bath towels, or the stuff that sits in your basement year after year? Right or wrong, most of our acquisitions and purchases are emotional first and then rationalized afterward.

Given all that we know about why people buy things and why they choose to take action to improve their lives, the first rule of marketing is this:

Your health-care solution must appeal to an emotion-based desire first.

You might think this is manipulation, but before you go there I want you to understand this important fact: Buying from an emotional place stems from biology. Our primary human instinct is to survive. In primitive times that meant we had to feed the belly, stop the bleeding, end the pain, and do all the other things necessary for us to exist so that nothing could get in our way of procreating our species. Therefore we became acutely aware of our physical state and would do everything we could to ensure optimal function. If something was amiss, our instincts would direct us toward a way to get back to homeostasis.

These instincts still remain today, residing within our limbic systems—our *reptilian brain,* and still drive decision-making in the human operating system. Therefore when your prospective patient is unwell and wants help, their primitive brain kicks in and steers their behavior. They want to stop the pain, have energy, survive, and even more—*thrive.* So they will immediately connect with your message if you speak to them where they live emotionally.

If you use logic, such as leading your communication with a dry recitation of your credentials, your mission, or your services, they will disconnect and go elsewhere for help. There is, of course, a time and place to highlight all of your "logical" accomplishments. Those are very important, too. But *leading* with them on your home page, in your conversations, and anywhere else you're promoting your services not only doesn't attract patients but can actually push them away.

The final reason that new marketing messages are so important is that when your message is clear, promoting your services becomes nearly effortless. The talks you give, the articles you write, the copy on your website, the programs and services you offer, the book you're writing—all of it lines up. You no longer frantically run around figuring out what you're about and how to position your work. When you understand the power of clear market messaging, you will be amazed at the freedom and control it brings to all your marketing activities.

Where Your Messages Matter Most

There are two primary messaging paths you will take to attract prospects to your practice: online and in person. The goal is to use a combination of both, because different people are attracted by different kinds of media, and a mix of both delivers the biggest bang for your buck.

Focus on places where your patients typically look for you. That is all that matters. Don't get caught up in following trends or cool new avenues to reach people. Your patients' behaviors should define the media you choose to promote your practice.

The online options include your website, blog, article marketing, video, and social media. In-person marketing includes talks and presentations, strategic alliances, networking, referrals, direct marketing, and print advertising.

Let's go through messaging strategies for each of these.

Website Messaging 101

I wish I had a dollar for every time I was told, "I just put up a brand-new website, but it's doing zilch to bring in new clients!" Once you get the general idea of messaging and a few other basics, building a compelling, engaging website is pretty simple. In case you're wondering, since it's highly likely that over 90 percent of your clients are going online to find you, and many people are skeptical of a business without one, *not* having a website isn't an option.

First you need a powerful home page. When a website visitor lands on your home page for the first time, they will spend less than *fifteen seconds* on your site before deciding whether to stay or to click away. If you don't engage them quickly and they leave, none of the other pages matter, do they? Your home page also has relevance to your other website pages, and I'll explain this further, too.

It's *Not* All about You

Don't take this personally, but a person in pain isn't all that interested in you—not at first. They first look to see if you get *them*. I cannot stress enough how important it is to make your home page less about you and more about your ideal client. Bottom line: Your home page should reflect the outcome that your niche market desires and your ability to deliver it.

The Seven Home-Page Messaging Essentials

Let's go through the seven most important things you can do right away to strengthen your home-page messaging (or create it). If you already have a website, incorporating these essentials shouldn't involve a whole lot of work.
The seven essential home-page messaging elements are:

1. **"In the right place" statement.** Your "in the right place" statement is essentially your tagline or slogan. What you want to communicate to your visitor is that they have arrived at the right location and have found the solution to their unmet need. These statements run the gamut, and you'll see lots of variations. But the ones that have the greatest impact are those that speak di-

rectly and clearly about whom you serve. Your visitor sho
"Yes! This gal's for me! She is speaking my language."

Examples of compelling taglines include:
- Weight management solutions for busy professionals
- Sleep better...naturally!
- Holistic sports performance solutions for weekend warriors
- Helping kids make the grades without the meds
- Safe alternatives for a healthy pregnancy and beyond
- Midlife without the crisis
- Healthy meals for busy families

Your tagline will change over time, so let your ideas flow in and
out as new things pop into your field of vision. (I'm on my sixth
tagline and counting.)

2. **Professional photo.** Are photographs also messages? You bet!
   In fact, we process images and graphics 60,000 times faster than
   text. One of the most powerful images on your home page is a
   professional photo of you. I know you're tempted to load up your
   home page with beautiful stock photos of vibrant, happy people
   running through fertile fields, flaxen tresses flowing in the wind,
   holding hands with their lovely children. But there are two problems with this: 1) it doesn't reflect the person coming to your website, and 2) people do business with real people, not with models.
   They want to see *you*. Do you look like someone they'd like to
   work with? Are you someone they can trust? Do the images on
   your website reflect warmth and connection? Remember you're
   trying to attract them, and that's pretty tough to do when they
   can't see what you look like the instant they land on your page. In
   those few seconds they spend on your home page, you want your

photo to be right there front and center; don't count on them staying around long enough to click on your "About" page to see what you look like.

The concept behind using your photo and not that of a model is based on the idea that the human face was the first "brand logo," a concept I learned from the book *The Human Brand*, by Malone and Fisk. They explain further that the face instantly conveys "identity, personality, intentions, and ability" all at once, and that people are drawn to—even crave—making this type of connection with you. So please put yours out there for the world to see.

Your photo should be taken by a professional photographer with great lighting and should be as recent as possible. It's fine if you want to use relevant stock photos and other images on your site, but don't use them in place of real photos of you, your clinic, your staff, your treatment rooms, or anything else that's in your practice, as they don't tell anybody anything about you or the experience they'll have when they come to see you. Be sure to put your personal headshot "above the fold" on your home page, which means that it doesn't require your visitor to scroll down to see it.

3. **Logo/name/phone.** It might sound crazy, but don't forget to include your logo, your name and/or business name, and phone number on your home page. Don't bury them. A professionally designed logo isn't essential; you can simply use your name, perhaps formatted in a cool font or special color to make it pop. Placing your phone number on the home page also makes it easier for someone to make the call to you versus forcing them to navigate throughout the site to find it.

4. **Testimonial/social proof.** Testimonials encourage people and help build trust. Nothing speaks louder than a satisfied client endorsing your services. This is powerful stuff, especially if you can get a testimonial from someone who is a local celebrity or has a position of authority or importance in your community. The key with testimonials, though, is to stay within HIPAA and FTC guidelines as they relate to your particular scope of practice. The details of how to keep out of trouble here could fill an entire book, but for many holistic health professionals it's illegal to use testimonials that include clinical data or improvement in specific, measurable results such as someone saying, "After visiting Dr. Smith I lost 12 pounds in 4 weeks!" In fact, the most compelling and safest testimonials are those that demonstrate a client's emotional transformation after working with you. Clients who talk about "having more energy to play with my grandkids" rather than "my lab result dropped from X to Y" are much more appealing. Remember my comments earlier about emotional messaging? That's the goal of a powerful testimonial. Focus on these and you won't get into trouble. I recommend a few rotating testimonials on your home page, and a separate testimonial page with a slew of them. Like all things with your business, seek the advice of an attorney to make sure you're compliant with HIPAA and FTC guidelines, as well as those of the state in which you practice.

5. **Niche market messaging: video or text.** I've covered messaging extensively, but when it comes to your home page your goal is to focus on the wants of your ideal client and give them *one single call to action* to start fixing their problem. Offer them a simple step to take to give them some hope. You can do this with text or video that essentially follows this outline:

- I understand what you are going through and how this is impacting your life.
- I can help you achieve the specific outcome you want.
- Get started today by signing up for my free gift (opt-in).

Remember, your home page content is not about you, your credentials, your mission, or your services; it must reflect your understanding of the desires of your ideal patient and how you can help them.

6. **Opt-in/call to action.** You might think that your goal on your home page is to get people to call for an appointment, but most marketing gurus claim it takes from seven to twenty exposures before someone decides to take action to meet with you. This concept is known as *effective frequency*, and most research shows that *fewer than three messages or exposures to you gets you nowhere, but a frequency beyond seven continues to have a cumulative benefit.* There are a few folks who are ready to call for an appointment right away (such as referrals), but the vast majority will not. So your absolute number-one goal with your website is to *collect interested visitors' email addresses for ongoing connection with them* (more on this in the next chapter).

This point is so important that I want to say it again: The number-one goal of your website is to collect email addresses. Very, very few people decide to buy something when they go to a website the very first time. Think about your own behavior if you need proof. An opt-in box allows you to collect a visitor's email address in exchange for something of value so you can continue to connect with them and keep the conversation going through emails and other communication vehicles. More communication equals more *exposures*; it builds the "know, like, and trust" factor and lets people get more comfortable with you so they will be more likely to set up an appointment when they're ready. I will be going into this idea in a lot more detail soon, but just remember to provide a single call to action—which should be to opt in to your list—right on your home page.

7. **Keep it simple.** Clutter leads to confusion. A home page with lots of links, calls to action, or an overwhelming amount of information to read turns off visitors and hastens a speedy exit from your site. Keep it clean, simple, and compelling, and give your visitor one thing only to do: opt in to your email list.

Essential Pages on Your Website

Your website should include at least the pages—and suggested messaging—listed below.

Home
Remember to focus your message on your target audience and not on you, and follow my guidelines in the prior section.

About
Here's where you are free to be all about you! That said, I strongly encourage you to not simply itemize your credentials, but to tell your story. In the wise words of Simon Sinek, people don't buy what you do; *they buy why you do it.* Remember my exercise from the "Purpose" section about writing your manifesto? Here is your opportunity to share that story—why you chose your profession and your passion to help people with the specific problem your niche market has. Be transparent about your struggle, your anger, your passion, or your desires. Let your visitors know that you

are a real, living, feeling human being. Malone and Fisk discuss how the true identity and character of a leader—and the warmth and competence of their brand—are conveyed best through the genuine story of their journey. That is a huge aspect that is often missing in the "About" section of many practitioner websites. Of course, you must also spell out your education, training, and any other credentials and experience that demonstrate you are highly qualified to help them.

Services/signature program

This page should outline your primary area of expertise and elevate your authority in your potential client's eyes. List your services, but more important, explain *how* the services you offer deliver the outcome your visitor wants to achieve. Enumerating the number of sessions, tests, and other elements that are included in your program doesn't tell prospects that your services will help them get better right now, and that's what they most want to know. In other words, describe how those six sessions, unlimited email, and discounts on supplements will deliver the results they want.

This brings up something I'm frequently asked: Should you list your prices on your website? If you're a direct-pay practice, your prospects will want to know how much your services cost. Whether you do that on your website or not is a personal decision; there's no right or wrong, and I've seen it both ways. Do what feels comfortable to you. I cover some strategies on dealing with costs and prices in the final section of the PEACE Process, which will help you position your prices, whether published or not.

Praise/testimonials

A separate page should be set up exclusively devoted to testimonials once you have collected at least a handful of them. I prefer the use of full names and photos of people who give you praise. Using initials or something even more vague can make these comments appear questionable; your visitor might wonder whether you fabricated them. If your client is unwilling to let you use their name, don't push it. Find others who will. Believe me; if they had great success with you they'll be more than happy to offer their name and even their photo. Pictures strengthen credibility and add interest, which engages site visitors.

Remember the HIPAA and FTC guidelines I discussed earlier? Since people are engaged by emotion rather than logic, it's easy to stay legal by having clients describe the changes in energy and love of life, and the things they can now do that they couldn't do before. Discussing improvements in lab numbers or pounds lost is risky; those things don't attract people anyway.

Keep in mind that most people are lousy at writing testimonials. You can guide them about what to say in order to keep it legal, or even offer to write it for them based on the comments they've made and ask them to edit or approve. They'll appreciate the guidance, and you have a much better chance of getting them to contribute and to highlight what matters most.

Contact/location

Believe it or not, I've seen practitioner websites that keep their location one of the biggest secrets on the planet! Make sure you put your business name, phone number, and contact form on a separate page under a "Contact" tab on your navigation bar. Don't bury it in your "About" or "Services" page! Even if you place it in the footer or header of all of your website pages, keep a separate "Contact" page on your site because people are used to looking for it there. Avoid publishing your personal email address on your website. There are robots that "scrape" websites for email addresses which can open the door for all sorts of crazy junk to land in your inbox. The better approach is to use a form that visitors fill out to get in touch with your office, possibly including a "captcha" code (those weird-shaped words that you type in a little box) that makes sure a human being is actually filling out the form.

And, of course, it must be said that you should monitor your inbox (and spam folder) regularly and respond ASAP to all legitimate inquiries.

Blog

In order for your website to stay relevant to search engines, you will want to continually add new, high-quality copy to it. A blog—whether you write once a week or once a month—shows search engines and visitors that your site is active and you're open for business. The content of your blog should incorporate everything discussed so far: niche-focused, emphasizing the outcome clients seek. Remember that authorship validates and elevates your expertise, and if you aren't doing some sort of writing on a regular basis it's more difficult to prove that you're the real deal. I'll be discussing the importance of authorship along with some tactics to start writing quickly later in the book.

Philosophy, Media, Speaking, Video pages

These pages—and others that you might have in mind—can be added if or as you desire. Most important, however, is that you avoid loading your site with lots of multilevel navigation, as this can be overwhelming and confusing to site visitors. Be mindful to include the things that absolutely must be on your website, especially from your visitors' perspective. This is not a dumping ground for your "stuff." It's a tool to help people learn about your work and whether or not you are someone they want to get in touch with. A confused mind clicks away, and when they're gone, they're usually gone for good.

You might be tempted to use cute or playful terms or something personal to you for your navigation tab labels. Please avoid this! When a person lands on your website—or any website for that matter—they are accustomed to seeing conventional navigation terms: Home, About, Services, Contact, Blog, etc. The last thing you want to do is irritate a potential client who is already feeling anxiety! Keep tab names very common and self-explanatory. Quirky or unfamiliar navigation terms are confusing to the average visitor and will do nada to attract and soothe people who are seeking help and comfort. Make your site easy for people to understand and find what they're looking for.

For the Multipractitioner Clinic

I'm often asked how to incorporate my website-building suggestions if you work in a practice with other clinicians, especially if there are multiple niches or multiple modalities being offered.

If your goal is to become an expert in your chosen field—to make a name for yourself and drive lots of business to your door—you should create your own independent website that links to the larger practice website. You don't need to spend a lot of cash on a website these days. Most multipractitioner sites are very poorly designed (unless they follow the PEACE principles), and you can't depend on a multipractice site to do much for you when it comes to attracting new clients.

Build your own brand and your own online presence. You are your own person; you're not just a part of an entity. Establish yourself accordingly with your specific messaging on a personal site. Not only will it elevate your role and place in the community, but it will help bring clients into the overall practice, too.

Never count on others to effectively market your services. You are the chief marketing officer for your brand and must always take control of putting your message out there the right way to the right people.

Messaging through Your Writing

Authorship establishes authority. The root word of *authority* is the Latin *auctoritas*, meaning "originator," which is the same root for the word *author*. So get comfy with writing.

At this point you might be thinking, "I don't like to write... must I do it anyway?" Notice that I'm not suggesting that you publish anything, although I hope you do. The real value in writing is much more about helping you (actually forcing you) put your thoughts and ideas together in advance; to consolidate your thinking so that all communication you share about your work makes sense to others.

Many in the holistic health field work by themselves in solo practices with little opportunity to bounce ideas off others. We live in our own heads—*a lot*. We think (and then speak) in terms that are meaningless to non-healers. We get excited when talking about our work and can overwhelm prospects by discussing concepts that frighten or confuse them. Writing provides structure and clarity for the myriad ideas floating around in that big brain of yours so that when it comes to outreach—from giving a talk to sharing your two-minute elevator speech—you've formulated your conversation ahead of time. This gives you much greater confidence so that you aren't stuck and won't stammer when it comes time to explain your work to others.

Of course, the biggest impact comes from sharing what you write with your prospects and clients. If your message is well-tuned and clearly linked to your niche's interests, the better it informs your content, especially your blog. The more consistently you communicate this message to your audience, the more they view you as an authority on the topic. That, in turn, engenders the "know, like, and trust" factor with you, which takes them one step closer to calling and setting up a consultation.

When you contribute your content to *other* websites is when things can really start to take off! Identify websites, newsletters, and media consumed by your ideal niche clients and see which are seeking content in your area of expertise. Many practitioners compete for space in the same standard websites, magazines, and publications that focus on health. I encourage you to think outside the box and make your mark where others rarely go. For example, if your practice caters to an affluent niche market, you might want to consider websites that sell products and services such as luxury cars and homes and vacation getaways. Perhaps they'd like to offer your top-of-the-line health solution to their readers in a special section of their newsletter? Differentiate yourself from your competitors and go off the grid instead.

Of critical importance is to create an *author's box*, a descriptor at the end of your article that directs people back to your website. Your author's box should not just be a laundry list of your credentials (remember the attraction principles!). Appeal to the unmet needs of your niche market. For example: "Mary Smith, NTP, is a functional nutrition expert who works with overwhelmed professional women who struggle to fit into their college jeans again and want to get back to their happy place. Learn more by picking up her free report at www.maryswebsite.com."

Don't sweat it or fret it if you can't write your way out of a paper bag. There are lots of freelance writing resources and virtual assistant firms (just type "virtual assistant help" in your search engine) that can connect you with ghostwriters, many of whom understand natural health. Maybe there's a community college or university in your city that has a writing program. If so, there will be students or interns who will write for you for a very reasonable fee.

If all else fails, either use a dictation application or invest in a transcription software program that allows you to dictate your articles into a computer headset and transcribes your thoughts directly into Microsoft Word in real time. You'll have to edit afterward, of course, but if you're better at talking than at writing—and who isn't—then a program like this might be your ticket.

I understand that you might be terrified of writing but do your best to work through it. It's the best way to establish authority, it is essential for SEO, and it strengthens your knowledge in your focus area. Don't let the admonishments of your fourth-grade teacher about your lousy writing skills instill doubt about your capabilities. Just sit down and start writing, and then hire a freelance editor to clean up your scribblings and give them a professional polish. Your clients come to you because they can't heal themselves. You are a clinician and a teacher. *Authoring* gives you *authority*, and it will pay off in more ways than you can imagine. And like most things in life, the more you write, the better you'll get at it.

General Guidelines for Writing

Length
- Ebooks: 3,000 words and up
- Blog posts: 300 to 2,500 words (longer is *usually* better for social shares and SEO, whereas shorter is *usually* better for getting comments from readers)
- Non-fiction books: 40,000 to 75,000 words (quality more important than quantity)

Depth
- Slice content thin; that is, don't write about inflammation, write about the benefits of turmeric.
- The longer the written piece, the deeper the content should go.
- Always keep your reader's abilities, interests, and knowledge in mind.

Style
- Give the what, the why, and the how-to.
- Use bullets and short sentences.
- Write in your voice. If you wouldn't use that word in speaking, don't use it in writing!

Titles and subtitles
- Keep titles bold and short, and use catchy concepts.

- Make subtitles more revealing, describing what the outcome of reading the content will deliver.
- Write the title first, then write the content, and then reread it to make sure the title fits.

Outcomes and tips
- Start by knowing what outcome you want your reader to walk away with.
- Don't just give information; give steps to take.
- Write about what your reader should think, feel, or do differently by the end of what they read.

Readability
- Make it fun, entertaining, inspirational, or engaging!
- Break through myths, provide new insights, and/or show your reader a new way to think about things.
- Use first person: I, me, we; and second person: you.

#1 writing tip: Model the works of others whom you admire! Don't reinvent the wheel.

Messaging with Video

Did you know that your videos can rank higher in search engines than your website? That's why it's important to not only use the proper keywords and phrases in your video titles, descriptions, and tags, but to also use these terms in your video scripts and transcripts that you upload alongside them.

Short, high-quality videos are the least utilized yet greatest opportunity to attract new patients. The key is to structure them in a compelling, simple way that delivers information your niche market wants. Unfortunately many practitioners use video to ramble on and on about their practice or health issues in general, which bores viewers to death. People are used to (and enjoy) watching videos that are entertaining and engaging.

One video structure I believe works well uses the following approach:

1. Acknowledge a problem or question that your patient has.
2. *Briefly* provide your expert opinion or big *aha!* to teach viewers about the problem.
3. Tell the viewer how to take one single, immediate step to find relief.

It's that simple. And it's easy to do in two minutes or less, which is about as long as anyone devotes to watching online video tips these days. Of course there are applications in which longer videos can work, but when you're creating simple patient-attraction videos, keep them short and sweet. Remember that the key is to weave that conversational terminology into your script, title, and description. Don't worry about creating professional quality video; focus on quality lighting instead (search YouTube to learn about three-point lighting), and use an external microphone to ensure the best possible sound.

The toughest challenge when it comes to having a strong on-camera presence is learning how to smile and talk as if the camera is a living, breathing human being. Just start rehearsing in front of a mirror. With just a little bit of practice you'll feel and look comfortable on camera and can set up your YouTube or Vimeo channel in no time.

Talks and Presentations

Giving public talks heads the list of things you can do to attract lots of new prospects and clients. There are two primary reasons for this. Number one, there is nothing more effective at building the "know, like, and trust" factor with strangers than standing up in front of them and showing that you are the real deal. Compared to being strictly an online entity, it's no contest. Because it takes people a long time to decide whether or not to buy something, you can significantly shorten the sales cycle by spreading your message of hope and healing through in-person appearances.

Number two, standing in front of a group of people in the spotlight instantly positions you as an expert or authority in their eyes. People are more likely to trust and believe whatever it is you have to say when you're behind the podium. After all, you wouldn't have been asked to present to them if you didn't know your stuff. Because one of your key attraction strategies is positioning yourself as an authority, talks and presentations should be pursued.

You can waste a lot of time, energy, and money giving public talks, though, so keep the following in mind:

1. **You need to benefit.** Your time is valuable and you should always be super focused on how and where you're spending it. If you can get paid to talk, that's great; however, that doesn't always happen unless you're a celebrity or have established yourself as an authority. Alternatively, find out if you're permitted to make an offer for your services at the end of the talk. If your host or sponsor will not let you sell from the stage, then ask if you can set up a table where people can meet with you after your talk so you can sell something to them. If neither of those options is available,

be sure you can get a list of attendees for ongoing marketing (see #4 below). If none of these are possible, then unless you need the rehearsal time I suggest you pass on the opportunity.

2. **Create one signature talk.** Prepare one presentation that leads people to buy your primary service or program, and use it every single time you speak. Of course, you should only talk to your niche market. Many practitioners waste huge amounts of time and energy creating countless presentations on a variety of un-related topics, and deliver them to audiences that have no use for their services. Not only does this create additional work, but in the end delivers very little in the way of new business. If you need the practice, feel free to accept requests to talk about other things to people outside of your niche market. But do not do this long term! Creating multiple presentations on topics that are outside of your focused niche market will negatively impact your valu-able, limited time and energy.

The objective of your talk is to tell your audience about the top three or four things they can learn, feel, or do as a result of listen-ing to you. You can create a variety of lengths for this talk so that it scales to the venue and audience needs, or you can take one small piece of your signature talk and make a complete talk out of it. *Your talks should always be some aspect of the same signature talk, and should always deliver value to your audience, regardless of length.*

3. **Structure Your Talk Effectively.** The human brain is ill-equipped to do the following things:
   a. **Listen, read, and comprehend at the same time.** Text-heavy PowerPoint slides that are read to an audience over-

whelm their brains' circuitry and cause them to disconnect.

b. **Absorb complex ideas.** Using the same medical terminology with your audience that you use with your peers distances you from them and puts them off.

c. **Connect the dots.** Loading up slides with complex data, studies, and graphs confounds a lay audience.

Choose your topic title by asking yourself, "What should my audience be able to do, learn, or feel at the end of my talk?" Get crystal clear on the takeaway and let that inform the first draft of your talk title. Then shape your talk and slides using these steps:

- Chunk your talk into *three or four key subtopics* that relate to your working title. That's about all the brain can retain when it comes to short-term memory and learning. Avoid including hundreds of slides that list every possible study or piece of data in the world! Sift and sort the content down to fit into only these few subtopics, with an eye toward creating a slide deck that contains the bare minimum of slides necessary to get your ideas across.

- Create your slides, making sure that each one is related to its subtopic. Test logic and flow by rehearsing your talk aloud. This simple activity ensures that what you are about to communicate delivers big impact. Tell them a story that connects the dots between your concepts and the outcomes they're looking for.

- For slides with text, use bulleted lists, quotes, and copy that someone can quickly scan and comprehend. Use graphics instead of text when appropriate. The title of each slide should be a complete thought, such as "Healthy Fats You Should Eat Daily"—not simply "Fats." Place your talking points in the notes section and *memorize* your talk! Slides are *not* a placeholder for every word you're about to say; they are to help your audience connect the dots between your words and your concepts. All eyes and ears should be riveted on you, not on the big screen.

4. **Always collect names and email addresses.** Not collecting names and email addresses is probably the biggest mistake you can make when giving a talk. Always come up with a strategy for collecting these. Since only a fraction of your audience will buy something at the end of your presentation, you want the opportunity to keep the relationship going through email communication so that when they're ready to see a practitioner you are top of mind.

There are lots of ways to do this. If it's a small audience, you can pass around a clipboard with a sign-up sheet and offer a free electronic gift in exchange for their email address, such as an outline of your talk or a recipe ebook that's relevant to your topic. Consider conducting a raffle or drawing. Regardless of the strategy you use, be sure to let your audience know that once they give you their email address you'll be emailing them health tips on occasion, so they don't feel like you're trying to trick them. Be transparent about how you'll be using their email address in the future, assure them that you will safeguard their information like a hawk, and let them choose whether or not they hand it to you. Don't be offended by those who don't sign up; you want only names of people who are interested in your services.

Your primary objective in giving a public talk is to build your list of email addresses, so if you forget or ignore this third step, you've missed a major opportunity and your presentation could be a waste of time. Yes, it's that important.

5. **Make a Compelling Offer.** If you've delivered a fabulous presentation, many people in the audience will be keen to work with you. Unless prohibited by your sponsor, offer one single service or program along with a deal if they sign up right away, such as a discount or bonus for those who take fast action that day. Don't promote every service, program, and product you have to the audience; this paralyzes listeners and prevents them from taking action. If an offer is not possible, don't sweat it. As long as you have collected email addresses, you have the opportunity to build ongoing relationships via your preferred communication method. In time, when they're ready to move forward with a practitioner, they'll think of you first.

Remember to always demonstrate above-and-beyond thanks to the sponsor who invited you to talk. This, of course, is just common courtesy. And it also puts you at the top of their list to invite back when they need a grateful and solid speaker.

Strategic Alliances

Messaging plays a big role when considering complementary practitioners or companies with whom you can form an alliance or partnership. As with article marketing, think outside the box—seek out others who likely cater to your niche market but aren't the usual suspects. For example, I know a nutrition expert who formed an alliance with a day spa that catered to the exact same niche market. They would hold open houses together, conduct special events on health and beauty, and share their lists with one another for ongoing marketing. It was a pretty creative way to get new business. Think of complementary businesses that might be a natural fit to reach your target audience. Just start with a strong sense of your niche market's demographics, hobbies, interests, and needs, and then think about who else might be targeting that niche market with services and products. That will lead you to some very unique partners, without a doubt.

Networking

If you're not focused, networking is another opportunity to waste precious time. Because few of us have a lot of extra bandwidth, it's crucial to target only those organizations and associations where you can find potential partners and/or possible prospects. Think about your niche. Look at areas of common interest and opportunities to build on your skills to determine whether or not an organization meets your needs for both personal growth and prospecting, speaking, etc.

There are a number of well-regarded professional networking organizations such as Business Network International (BNI), LeTip, American Businesswomen's Association, Entrepreneur's Organization, National Association of Women Business Owners (NAWBO), and other options to explore, like mastermind groups, your chamber of commerce, and even groups at Meetup.com. Simply do your research and ensure that the group you choose to get involved with has a decent structure in place for regular meetings, facilitates exchange of referrals between its members, adheres to quality standards and ethics, and gives everyone equal consideration so you don't have to fight for (or pay extra money to get) attention.

The word *work* is in the word *network*; it's not enough to just show up, meet people, and exchange business cards. *Follow-up* is paramount when it comes to forming lasting relationships. Be careful not to contact people only when you need them or their help. Make it a constant and ongoing activity in your business development strategy and it will pay big dividends over time.

Referrals

Few things are as effective as referrals from those who trust you and have had success working with you. The *2013 Nielson Global Survey of Trust in Advertising* showed that word-of-mouth recommendations from friends and family are still the most influential type of advertising. Eighty-four percent of global respondents across fifty-eight countries said that referrals from friends were the most trustworthy source of information. Likewise, the *Nielsen Survey* showed that people are four times more likely to buy when referred by a friend. The concept behind referrals is known as *social proof,* which means that when someone recommends you, it carries greater credibility than any other form of advertising. That's why testimonials have so much impact.

The problem with referrals is that while many people might say they will refer others to you, most of them don't. I was floored to learn that although 83 percent of people are willing to refer after a positive experience, only 29 percent actually do!

Whether it's because they're too busy or they just don't know how to promote you, referrals often fall short of what they could be. But it's not the fault of your client. They simply need help to articulate what you do. So give them the right words to say. You can write out an email or create a letter and forward it to them so they can pass it along to others. Use your messaging in the copy that you write. Whatever you do, don't leave this to chance; help them help you.

Reward those who refer you to others with deep gratitude, or as I call it, "gratitude with impact." Don't just shoot a generic form email that says "thanks a lot for the referral." Impact means take them to lunch, send them flowers, send them a book they might like, or deliver a handwritten personal thank-you note. It's not a bribe but rather a little unexpected gift of thanks post-referral. Not only will this reward you with more referrals, but it's the right thing to do.

Steps to Set Up a Referral Framework

1. Identify three *centers of influence* (COIs):
   - Clients: Who has had success with you? Who raves about you? Who do you like?
   - Tier 1 referrals: Professionals in your industry; allied health professionals
   - Tier 2 referrals: Friends; family; personal/professional associates outside of your industry such as your attorney, accountant, hair stylist, dentist, bookkeeper, etc.

2. Create your reward and recognition program. Options might be:
   - Discounts, free services, gift cards, health-conscious gifts
   - Thank-you notes and cards
   - Donations to charity
   - Flowers, gifts, lunches for tier 1 and 2 referrals

Remember, these are not bribes to incentivize clients to refer people to you, but rather unexpected gifts of gratitude to be given to them after their referral comes calling.

3. Script your referral materials (conversations and emails/letters) per below:

Scripting your referral conversations with clients

> Does your referral conversation sound like this: "Hey Liz, by chance would you know someone who could benefit from my services?" Liz ponders and eventually says, "Well, not off the top of my head, but I'll keep thinking about it." This is how 90 percent of referrals are requested, and unfortunately, rarely if ever will this result in a positive response because it's not the right question! It's too broad, too non-specific for people to effectively answer.
>
> Clients need a frame of reference to help them narrow down the playing field of potential referral candidates. Try this instead:
>
> 1. Have your client acknowledge the benefit you provided.
> 2. Ask them if they have friends, relatives, and associates who might be experiencing the same problems or have the same desires. Review the gist of your core niche-statement message with your client.
> 3. Remind your client that if they appreciate the relationships they have with those who share the same issues and who stand to benefit in the same way your client did from working with you, then it seems the neighborly, loving, right thing to do to at least put them in touch with you and let them decide for themselves if what you offer is right for them, too.

Instead of focusing on getting your client's help, you have switched the focus to how they might help their friends get well.

Scripting your referral conversations with tier 1 and 2 referrals

Here's how you might start the ball rolling with allied professionals and your friends and personal COIs:

> "John, you're a member of the Lawyer's League here in Phoenix, right?" [Confirm]
>
> "Do you go to their meetings on a regular basis?" [Confirm]
>
> "Is there anyone in your association who might be dealing with the same issue/interest as you and might benefit from my services? Maybe one or two people you've known in the group for a while or sit next to regularly?"

You've given John a narrow frame of reference from which he might "see" the potential referrals in his mind. Be sure to review your core message with him: who you are, what you do, and whom you serve. Ask if he would like some of your business cards to pass out at the next meeting; or better yet, if the group might have any interest in a presentation by you. Consider asking for some of John's cards to give to associates or clients of yours to demonstrate reciprocity. No matter what, never push or hand over a stack of cards without John eagerly reaching for them! This should always be a low-pressure conversation for you both.

Direct Marketing

One promotional area I'm often asked about is direct marketing. With all of the rush to online marketing, it's interesting to note that snail mail is making a comeback and some practitioners are seeing positive results with it. There are very specific ways to do it correctly, however, and keep in mind that it's not going to be as cost-effective as online strategies. But it's now easier than ever before.

The U.S. Postal Service has a direct mail service that provides a simple way to target a specific zip code area with a promotional campaign. If your niche market can be targeted from a geographic standpoint, such as an affluent community or a market within a set distance from your office, this can be a great way to go. Just head to your local post office to learn more. If you do have a solid mailing list for your existing clients and prospects, you can use that... or even a combination of your list plus the USPS service, if you wish. A few things to consider:

True promotion: When you send direct mail, be sure to announce a true promotion and not just that you are open for business. A piece of mail that says, "Hey, I'm here, come visit me," will do very little in the way of enticing people to take action. The mail should offer a discount, a special service, or something unique *that has a time limit or expiration date* to motivate people to come visit you sooner rather than later.

Lumpy mail: You can make your direct mail stand out from the rest of the mail by using an odd-shaped or colored envelope or stuffing a padded mailer with some little trinket or trifle. This is a concept that has been recommended by direct-mail guru Dan Kennedy. Your goal is to get people to open your mail by making it intriguing or mysterious—a curiosity. You can find all sorts of fun envelope-stuffers by searching under "logo gift items," or head to one of those dollar stores. All you need is an inexpensive item related to your service, or to the letter itself, that would thrill or otherwise grab the attention of your recipients. For example, I once stuffed a cheap kitchen timer into an envelope with a letter, the first line of which said, "Would you mind taking just one minute of your time to read this? I've even included a timer with this letter to help you keep track." I was amazed at the response that generated!

Multiple mailings: Be prepared to send multiple mailings to the same people. Remember, it takes seven or more exposures to your product or service before someone will decide to buy it. And if you're relying strictly on direct mail, you'll need to plan for a minimum of three mailings over a short period of time. Of course, here's where the cost of mailings can soar, but they can work if done well.

Combine marketing media: Why not launch a big campaign using multiple marketing tactics? This approach can support a direct-mail campaign very well. For example, you might conduct an email marketing campaign and reinforce it with an ad in a local paper, a social media campaign, and a direct-mail piece (or several) in order to increase your chances of reaching your market in the way(s) they might be looking for you. This is a pretty advanced tactic of course, but it's quite effective. And if you have a large list of inactive clients, it can be a great way to get out in front of them and get them back in the door. Ideally there is a fair amount of overlap between your email list, address list, and social media followers. That's the tricky part. But if this sounds like something you want to take on, it can be a powerful marketing play.

Print Advertising

Let's talk print advertising for a moment. Print ads aren't cheap, and unless you're promoting in a medium that is very targeted to your list, they will generate limited returns. There are some exceptions to this, especially if you live in a small community where everyone reads the same media. But keep in mind that, like direct-mail advertising, print advertising also has its greatest impact if done multiple times. It's a shotgun approach, and I'm not a huge fan of it, but in small, tightly defined markets it can work. If you're already using it with some success—and by that I mean the dollars you are spending are more than made up with new, lifelong patients—then keep doing it.

Above all else, test. Don't guess when it comes to direct-mail and print advertising. Start with a small budget and decide for yourself if it's worth the time, energy, and money to go this route.

Business Listings: Google, Yelp, and More

Want some free advertising? It can't get any easier (and certainly not any cheaper!) than setting up your business profile on Google and Yelp, two well-used and trusted sites. I'm actually surprised by how many people completely forget about these simple platforms when it comes to establishing their community presence.

Many people fear that if they list at these sites their clients will post bad reviews and comments. That is always possible, of course, yet there are ways to report spam and to respond to any comment—good or bad—you receive. You will need to decide for yourself if you are willing to manage your listing closely for such things. What's way worse than negative feedback is a business that does not *respond* to feedback at all. I find that when I view negative remarks on a Yelp or Google business page, if the business apologizes and offers some sort of remedy, I view that business very positively. After all, sometimes a business owner is unaware that a customer has had a bad experience. I think it's better to be aware of a client problem and resolve it than to be in the dark about an issue and get bad press behind my back. But that's me.

To learn how to set up your free listing, simply search for "Google business profile" and "Yelp business listing" for all the details. Be sure to follow their instructions to create the highest-quality listing possible.

5. Connect

This step is where the magic happens—making deep connections with your prospective patients and clients and keeping the good vibes going with your existing ones.

To this point I've been focused on your strategic play: identifying your purpose, determining which market you will work with, and spreading your message of hope and healing far and wide. These strategies will put you on the map in your community. But it's this next step, *connect*, that guides people one step closer to getting onto your appointment book. The phrase "If you build it they will come" only works in the movies. In marketing a holistic practice, the more accurate statement is "If you build *relationships* they will come."

The average person needs to know, like, and trust you before they decide they're ready to work with you. These factors develop as a result of learning about you in some way, such as hearing you speak, reading your book, seeing your website, hearing your name, finding your Facebook page—somehow getting in front of them in a favorable light multiple times.

This is especially true when it comes to a health-care practitioner. Your prospective clients are suffering and will be sharing some very intimate details with you. Their problems might be embarrassing or frightening to them. It's one thing to trust a car salesman when you're purchasing an automobile; it's another to bare your soul, pour your heart out, and admit failings and personal tragedy to a complete stranger. Trust is absolutely essential. They have to feel safe; they need to know they can open up to you. That's why testimonials and referrals are so very, very important. Social proof accelerates trust and credibility like mad! But you still need to do *your* part to ensure confidence on the part of your prospective client.

Since your ideal client is not very likely to call you up following their first website visit, how well your site converts visitors into clients isn't always the best metric. The better metric when it comes to website effectiveness is how well it captures visitors' email addresses so you can take the next step and *connect with them*. If you've done a great job with your messaging, your visitor knows they are in the right place, and while they might not be ready to buy right then, they are ready to connect and hand over their email address *as long as you give them a compelling reason and a simple way to do so*. They will trade their most precious thing, their email address, only if you offer them something they really, really want.

Collecting Email Addresses with an Opt-In Box

This point bears repeating: *The number-one goal of your website is to collect email addresses.* And the best way to collect email addresses is with an opt-in box, something you've seen frequently but is often poorly done.

When you deliver talks, write articles, or go to networking events, your primary action item is to get the contact information of prospects, in particular their email addresses, so you can continue to communicate with them and begin to develop the oh-so-important connection. When a business is for sale, the first thing a prospective buyer (or financial institution) asks about is the size of the client list and prospect list, because without a list there is no opportunity to sell anything to anyone. Your most valuable business asset is your list. Without it your practice is dead in the water.

The good news is that with an automated opt-in on your website, collecting this information is simple as long as you give them something of value in return for their contact information. This is called the law of reciprocity. Give generously, give great value, and you shall receive great things in return.

We need only look back at our ancestors once again to understand the mechanism behind why this works. As early humans we relied on one another's skills to trade services. If you grow veggies, I'll hunt and trade you small game in exchange. If you make tools, I'll make pottery and we'll trade. It was through reciprocation and trading that societies and communities evolved and blossomed as they did. The goal of an opt-in is to trade something that your website visitor considers to be valuable in exchange for their contact information.

I often get pushback from practitioners on the website opt-in strategy. They share that they personally hate those annoying pop-ups or "tricks" to extract an email address and abhor the thought of doing this on their own sites. But what you might not like has nothing to do with what your ideal client wants. You are not them! When you create something valuable for them to sign up for, you aren't being underhanded in any way; you're offering them something of value that they want—something that gives them insight, help, or ideas they truly desire.

Please don't make the mistake of inviting visitors to sign up for a free newsletter or ongoing tips and announcements. This is not effective. I don't know anyone who hands off their email address because they want to receive more things to read, do you? Giving people more to do in their already busy lives demonstrates that you're out of touch with reality. Newsletter sign-ups aren't valuable because they just aren't unique these days. I'm not opposed to sending newsletters, and they can have a place in your practice, but they are rarely considered a desirable trade for an email address.

When your website visitor signs up for your free gift, they're added to your email marketing list. Communicate with those on your list regularly in order to increase your impressions, or exposures, and build a connection. If you give visitors a valuable opt-in gift that they like, they will be more willing to read your email later on.

The opt-in box is typically found on the home page, though many sites include one on every page. It ideally sits above the fold.

The most effective opt-in boxes have these elements:

- Heading that summarizes the benefits of the gift
- Picture or other graphic
- Email address and name fields
- Call to action—namely, to opt in to receive your free gift
- Privacy policy
- Statement that they will receive ongoing tips and ideas from you every so often

Step 1: Trade Valuable Content for Visitors' Email Addresses

People like free stuff, but it must be perceived as valuable. When your visitor comes to your site they immediately see your opt-in box along with an invitation to give you their email address in exchange for a valuable gift. For example, you might offer them a free three- to five-page after-school healthy snack guide to help busy moms quell kids' hunger pangs before dinner is ready. You might create a quiz that helps them determine whether or not they have a specific issue such as gluten sensitivity. Ebooks from thirty to fifty pages are also a very nice gift to give people. Or you can record a thirty- to sixty-minute audio file on a topic that your niche struggles to understand, have it transcribed, and offer both the audio and the transcription together as a free gift. Some people offer a video training series where over the course of a couple of weeks prospective clients receive a two- to ten-minute training video from you every couple of days or so, perhaps sharing natural remedies for seasonal sniffles.

In order to make your opt-in call to action stand out, eliminate all other distractions on the home page. Don't overwhelm your visitor! Make it very clear what action they should take and why they should do it right away; that they'll be able to make progress toward something they want: stop the pain, sleep better, have better energy—whatever it is you are offering your niche market. If you've done your research and you know what your niche market wants, creating this message should be pretty simple. Your call to action is to have visitors opt in for a "free gift" that takes them one step closer to that outcome. It might sound weird to tell visitors what to do, but when people come to your website they often need some focus and direction. Your opt-in call to action gives them that focus.

As you create your gift, here are some rules you should follow:

Gifts should:

- **Speak to the outcome for your niche market.** Be sure your gift delivers something that takes your visitor closer to the outcome they want.

- **Provide immediate value.** Get to the bottom line fast and give them a small step to take right away. Giving out volumes of stuff is not nearly as important as delivering simple and valuable help. In fact, given our attention-span-of-a-gnat society, less can most certainly be best.

- **Provide quick results.** You want them to have some small success with your gift, some new awareness that makes them say, "Wow! She really knows her stuff." This sets you up as someone they can trust and ultimately enlist for help down the road. And if you've done a great job with your opt-in gift, they might just call you sooner rather than later. Your gift should recommend a single, small step they can take to experience an immediate result. Perhaps it's a short script for a mindful meditation that calms them. Or advice for eliminating one single food to help them avoid bloating. The faster they see improvement or gain insight, the more willing they will be to stay connected with you.

- **Demonstrate generosity.** Give of yourself generously! Don't be concerned that they won't need you if you give them all the answers. Most of their problems have been going on a *long* time, and your simple guide will not fix them. And if it does? Hallelujah! That's one more person you've helped to heal.

Gifts should *not*:

- **Be a newsletter.** I explained above why a newsletter is a bad idea for a gift. They aren't immediately delivered, they aren't special (they are ubiquitous!), and rarely does someone sign up for generic things to read delivered via email. They want immediate relief for their specific problem.

- **Sell anything.** Minimize selling your services through your gift. You are building a relationship; don't ask a stranger to marry you right after your first date! They need multiple exposures to you to trust you. If you start to sell too soon, they might feel that you have betrayed or tricked them, and disconnect. Be patient about selling; now is not the time. They know that your services are for sale; they'll call when they're ready.

- **Be about you.** This is not the place to brag about yourself either. Your website provides all the information they need to learn about you. No need to put that in your opt-in gift.

- **Trick or betray people.** Your opt-in gift is about demonstrating compassion, warmth, and competence. It's about providing insight and inspiration to a complete stranger. It's from this place that true connection can blossom.

Step 2: Make the Email Connection

Now that you've been driving people to your website with your various outreach activities and have captured their email address through your opt-in gift, the second step in the process of connection is to start a conversation.

There are two primary ways to communicate with those on your email list. The first is through your ezine and/or your blog. These should primarily be used to inform, educate, and build relationships with those on your list. Provide insights and actions that help your audience improve their lives, giving them ideas and hope. You can include graphics or other visual aids to support your articles. The purpose of these tools is to develop the "know, like, and trust" factor between you and your audience.

An ezine can be a single article that gets to the point *fast*. There's no need to write multiple articles or use fancy ezine templates that take a lot of time to put together. Alternatively you can send out a very brief and compelling announcement about your recent blog post and direct your readers to your website to read it. In either case, respect your reader's time. Avoid dragging them through lots of non-essential content just to reach a specific word count. Give them the bottom line as simply as you can in order to get your point across. Above all, avoid constantly promoting your business! These are tools for educating and building relationships with your audience and establishing your expertise. You can occasionally announce an upcoming event or program in an ezine, but don't get into the habit of using an ezine as a promotional mechanism. If your regular communication always pushes your audience to buy something or to come in for an appointment, readers will grow weary and in short order they will either stop reading what you send to them or unsubscribe altogether. They'll assume that your only goal is to sell to them. It's tough to create deep, loyal, trusting relationships if they feel your only goal is to get their money!

I recommend sending an ezine or blog-post announcement one or two times a month. This ensures that your audience remembers you, stays engaged, and keeps your name at the ready when it's time to get help.

The second type of email communication is what I call "solo promo emails." They consist of one topic, have a single purpose, and are exclusively about selling something to those on your list. Use plain text—no graphics or photos—and write a clear call to action that invites people to buy something. Be careful not to send solo promo emails too often. Four to six times per year is sufficient. Be sure to announce a *true promotion* such as a special deal, offer, discounted price, or something new and exciting that's happening in your practice. There should be a time limit, too, on how long the offer lasts, to drive immediate action; otherwise they'll wait. And wait. And forget to act on it. Inviting people to come in for their regular visit does not constitute a promotional email unless you're giving them a special reason and time frame in which to take action.

Let's go over a few email communication rules:

1. **Use compelling subject lines.** The single most important aspect of email communication is to create a subject line that makes people want to open your mail. After all, if they don't open it, what's the point? You're looking for a "high open rate"—a high percentage of those on your list who open the email. An example of a boring subject line is "May Newsletter, Volume 4, issue 2." An example of a compelling subject line is "Four little-known secrets for kicking the gluten habit." Which would *you* rather open?

Create a *swipe file* in which you collect emails that have great subject lines that you might be able to model for future purposes. Then any time you're stuck you can grab your swipe file and get some quick ideas. Remember, the operative word here is "model."

It's not cool (or legal) to copy anyone else's materials verbatim.

2. **Get to the point!** People are busy. Make it easy on them by creating ezines and emails that are easy to read, have lots of white space and bullets, and don't go on endlessly with a lot of fluff. Respect your readers' time. State your key point early in the article and entice them to read more for the details. People scan when they read; write your copy accordingly.

3. **Always provide benefits, actions, or outcomes.** Write with your niche market in mind and make sure your content gives them great value. Discuss things they're interested in, not what you want to tell them. If you're educating them about how a specific food supports brain health, for example, be sure to speak in lay terms, not medical jargon. Give them an action to take such as how to shop for that food, how to prepare it, or a new way to eat it. People can find almost any kind of information they want on the web; your job is to give them a new or different way to think about it that they otherwise wouldn't consider, to demystify and simplify it, and to deliver the information in a way that they most want to receive it.

4. **Speak to one person at a time.** This point applies to all the communication you put out there. Even in a crowded conference room, each person is participating as an individual with their personal concerns. Whether it's your website, an email, or even a presentation, conduct a personal conversation between you and one single person who is listening to you.

Do You Have Permission to Send Email to Others?

Leadership isn't a position that you take, it's something you earn. According to leadership expert John Maxwell, "If you have integrity with people, you develop trust. The more trust you develop, the stronger the relationship becomes. The better the relationship, the greater the potential for a leader to gain permission to lead."

That's why growing a base of followers—and marketing to them—is best accomplished with their express consent. *Permission marketing*, a term coined by Seth Godin, is the single most powerful method of filling your practice with long-term, loyal clients who will follow you anywhere.

Willingly giving someone your email address gives them permission to send future emails to you. That's the essence of permission marketing. Whether it's for a webinar, an opt-in gift, a health summit, or even at a public talk, when someone gives you their email address they are essentially raising their hand and communicating that they are interested in your ideas.

I'm a strong proponent of building your list and developing deep connections with your followers through permission marketing. It's the most effective (and cost-effective) way to establish leadership in your field and to grow your practice with the people you want to work with and—maybe more important—*with those who want to work with you.*

Your list of prospects and clients who choose to align with you is your key practice asset. You can have all the healing talent in the world, but if you have no followers to share your gifts with, your ability to have an impact suffers. Receiving valuable information from you allows your audience to get to know, like, and trust you. And since it takes a long time for people to feel comfortable enough to decide to work with you, an ongoing email conversation facilitates and accelerates this trust-building process.

People who sign up for your list are telling you they like what you have to say—they're willing to hand over their email address in exchange for the value you're giving them. They *want* what you are providing. And as long as you continue to provide value in your future communication with them, they'll likely hang around long enough to ultimately exchange their money for your services. That's how email marketing plays a key role in building your authority and your client base.

Of course you must never email people without their permission. In fact, consent is not only common courtesy; most countries' email marketing laws stipulate that people need to give you permission to email them in order for you to send them campaigns.

There are generally two types of permission: implied permission and express permission. Implied permission involves those with whom you have an existing relationship, perhaps a current client or active member of your website membership program. If you don't have implied permission to email someone, then you'll need express permission. Express permission is granted when someone specifically gives you permission to send them email, potentially by entering their email address in an opt-in form on your website or signing up for a webinar or for a raffle at a talk.

Collecting names or business cards from people and then plugging them into your email marketing system without their knowledge should never be done! It is rude and wrong. Do not send broadcast emails to someone who hasn't specifically opted in or signed up at an event at which you have clearly stated that they are being added to your email list. Even your clients, friends, and business associates are off limits without implied or express permission.

There are laws in many places that also require you to provide a way for people to unsubscribe from your mailing list with each email you send out. Since I know I always have the option to unsubscribe, I'm willing to sign up for things that might help me. I don't worry too much about handing over my email address because the power to disconnect is always in my control. It's your choice whether or not to roll the dice and trade your email address for the potential reward in return. The same thing goes for whether or not you wish to build your own list in this manner.

Either way, fretting over this strategy is futile because, like it or not, permission-based marketing will be around for a long time to come, and when done well it ignites organic growth for your practice and your position in the community.

Step 3: Social Media Strategy

Social media is a beast that deserves a lot more space than I'm willing to provide here. It's morphing rapidly, and anything I write will likely be out of date by the time this book reaches your hands. That said, there are some general social media guidelines that at this point in time seem to be holding true even as platforms, algorithms, and much more shift beneath our feet.

The most important thing I want to convey is this: *Social media is not your starting place, but something that comes after you have developed your opt-in on your website and your niche-focused marketing message.* This statement probably flies in the face of what you may have heard from others. But I have yet to find any integrative or holistic health-care practitioner who has made a killing by starting out their marketing efforts exclusively with social media.

Social media is an important component in building and maintaining relationships with those in your community. It does not replace, but rather supports the rest of your marketing efforts and plays an important role in today's connected environment. Unless you work with an audience that was born before the 1940s you will want to consider some form of social media presence, as your audience will likely look for you there.

While social media is an important player in your overall marketing scheme, it is a lousy way to conduct any sort of ongoing, meaningful conversation with prospects and patients. It's hard to know when or if your audience is online when you post your pearls of wisdom. Social media algorithms change regularly, and your latest group announcement may not even show up in your followers' news feeds. That's why, as with all other marketing outreach, a primary goal of social media is to build an opt-in list that you can manage yourself. Having those names on your email list increases your odds of building connection through your ezine and/or blog. Not only does this allow you to maintain more control over the conversation, but it is still proven to be more effective at generating revenues for non-celebrities than social media.

Whether it's Facebook, Twitter, LinkedIn, Instagram, You-Tube, Pinterest, or whatever new platform might surface, your main objective on social media is to educate, entertain, engage, and build connection with your followers. Depending on your style, you might want to post things that are a little bit funny or edgy. Maybe you prefer to alarm or shock, or maybe you wish to inform and educate. Whatever your style, the goal is to get people to occasionally return to your website and opt in to become part of your list so you can continue to build relationships with them. As far as selling is concerned, the general rule of thumb is to devote only a fraction—perhaps 5 percent—of your social media posts to promotional messages. Just as with your ezine, if you become a selling machine on social media, people will find you annoying and disconnect from you.

Which social media platform is right for you? That depends on where your niche market hangs out; wherever that is, start there. At a minimum you will probably want to have a Facebook and/or Instagram page, and a LinkedIn account for developing professional relationships and alliances. If you are keen to use video, visit YouTube and check out what others in your profession are creating. You'll immediately discover that there is plenty of room for high-quality videos for your niche market! Two-minute tips videos that educate your niche market are very popular and exploding in popularity given our devotion to consuming content via mobile devices.

No one is a natural at video—it takes a bit of practice to get comfortable with it. Start rehearsing today, and within a short while it'll be a snap. Plus, as a Google property, YouTube videos have a strong built-in SEO element that can help your search-engine ranking.

As far as other platforms, do your research, yet don't spend too much time on social media until you've built your foundation: your niche, your website, your opt-in, and your email marketing vehicles. Yes, you need to have a presence, but you can waste a lot of time browsing and pondering what to post and where, and the next thing you know hours of your life have slipped by. Once you've selected the one or two social media platforms to focus on, limit yourself to ten minutes in the morning and ten minutes in the afternoon *for business only*. Do your personal social media work during your time off. Some people use automatic scheduling software such as Hootsuite, but don't rely on such programs exclusively. They can appear robotic when used too much, because they push and don't interact with your audience. Remember, social media is about being social!

6. Engage

It's time for your final step: Engaging and enrolling prospects to become loyal clients and patients. This is where you shift your focus from *marketing* to *selling your services*.

The first four steps of the PEACE Process cover marketing strategies, which typically involve a one-to-many approach in which you deliver your core message to a lot of people in a general way. It is a strategic, long-term effort that presents awareness of your market position to a targeted audience. The goal of marketing is to open avenues of opportunity. You are broadly announcing to your niche market, "I understand what you're going through and offer solutions to help you achieve your desired outcome."

The goal of selling is to convert a prospective patient into a paying one; it primarily involves one-to-one contact with a single individual to get them to exchange money for your services. The message to your targeted prospect is "I know what you specifically want and here is how you can pay me to get it."

You might feel uneasy about words like *close, deal, convert,* and other sales-y terms. But unless you're running a charity or you're living off your family's trust fund, there's no way around the fact that you must provide your services in exchange for money. Remember my analogy about your practice being like a solid rock upon which you stand so that you can throw a life preserver to the person floundering in the waves? Establishing your rock requires cash.

If you're hesitant about ensuring that your financial needs are met, you won't last very long as a practitioner. As a successful practitioner you wear lots of hats. One of those hats is that of an entrepreneur—a business owner. That means you must become comfortable with encouraging people to trade their money for your help.

Let's take a little side trip into the world of sales. The philosophy of selling has done an about-face in recent years. Since everyone has access to information on the web, the sales conversation no longer needs to be about spelling out every single possible detail of your services. Today's consumers (your clients) are much savvier. They come into your office with more knowledge than ever before. They don't want to be sold to; they want to buy a future outcome that they desire. This makes your work much easier.

Sales effectiveness begins with understanding what people want. Nobody comes to you because they want to buy your services; they seek you out because they want to stop their pain and end their suffering. So focus on the *outcome* your prospect wants early in your sales conversation with them, and not on the *solutions* that you offer. If you explain your solutions too soon, there's a good chance you will sell them something they don't even want. You can't know what they want unless you first get out of your head and into theirs.

Most of the clients who come to you did not develop their issues overnight, and if they did there are doctors and clinics more suitable to help them with acute care needs. You work with clients who have chronic issues, and resolution does not come in the form of a pill or emergency surgery. Your therapy requires a shift in behavior and a change in mindset. Making your clients comfortable with this mindset shift requires some new guiding principles about sales.

PACE: The Prospect-to-Patient Sales Method

I developed the PACE Sales Method to take you through four key steps to help your clients envision the future outcome they want to reach and choose *you* to help them get there. The four steps are Prepare, Ask, Clarify, and Enroll.

I call this PACE not just because it's a nifty acronym—although it is—but because the word itself suggests steady progress at a constant rate. When you pace yourself, you adopt the forward speed that works for you and that you can sustain over the long term. The key is to keep the transition from prospect to paying patient comfortable for both of you, while remembering that your mission is to help your fellow human being lead a happier and healthier life. But you can't do this for them; they need to believe in the value of your services and say, "Yes, let's move ahead."

The six guiding principles of PACE are:
1. Help people get what they want, not what they need.
2. Move people, don't manipulate them.
3. Focus on outcomes, not solutions.
4. Ask, don't explain. Listen, don't talk.
5. Dig deep for clarity.
6. Play to your strengths.

Keep the process slow and steady. Take the time to understand how it is you can help an individual make progress toward the things they want. In the heat of your zeal to heal someone you can tend to race through all the possible ways you can help them and in the process overwhelm and ultimately frighten them off.

By following the four steps below, you'll be able to understand the perspective of the person you're speaking to and have much greater control over the outcome of the conversation. And, of course, get new patients and clients.

1. Prepare

The most important thing you can do when you begin a conversation with a prospective client is to shut out everything else going on around you. Prior to the meeting, if possible, gather all the information you have about the individual: their issues, history, and what they're looking for from you. That takes a fair amount of focus and requires that you be other-centered. Spend just a few minutes thinking about nothing else but the conversation you're getting ready to have. Stop checking your email, text messages, and anything else that's going on in your business, and shut out assumption and judgment. Instead, open your heart so you can be calm and receptive. Respect the fact that an individual is hurting and wants help. Having this sense of "beginner's mind" before uttering one word to your prospect can be a powerful way to feel in control and confident about how to guide the conversation.

2. Ask

Ask your prospect for information—and listen to the answers they give! Many people think that selling is all about talking, and nothing could be further from the truth. The best salespeople in the world will tell you that selling is about asking powerful questions and carefully listening to not only what is answered, but what *isn't* being said. It's hard to hear either of those if you're yammering away. This part of the process is about asking questions with two key goals:

1. Finding out if there's a match between their needs and your services (qualifying your client)

2. Gauging their level of interest, pain, and desire for transformation

Avoid the temptation to sell them anything until you understand what they want. Be patient with your questioning. This is not the time to solve their problem. They first want to talk to someone who will sincerely listen to them. Here are my top questions for this step of the PACE Sales Method:

- What brings you here today?
- What have you tried before that worked? What didn't work?
- What outcome are you looking for?
- What interests you most about my service?
- What more would you like to know about me?
- What will you need to know, have, or do to decide to move forward with me?
- What questions do you have?

Remember to ask your question and then be quiet. *Listen.* Give your client time to think and answer. Base your next question on their answers to the previous questions. Repeat their response back to them to show you're listening. For example, if they express hesitation about your fee, gently say, "I understand completely that you have some concerns about affordability. That need not be an obstacle to your good health. We offer a payment plan that might be a good solution for you. Would you like to learn more about it?"

3. Clarify

Clarification is a powerful step in the process that many practitioners forget to take before offering their solution. Remember, PACE yourself. Dig a bit deeper into how this problem is impacting your prospect's life. Allow them the opportunity to emotionally connect with their problem and understand how, exactly, it might be impacting not only them but their friends, their family, and their work. While you might think these are difficult or awkward things to talk about, once you get comfortable with them you will find that people generally delight in the clarity it brings to them about their problems.

Asking the questions below allows you to identify the fears, obstacles, and resistance your prospective client might have in working with you. This is crucial to understanding and can help you position your solution. I have rarely seen people use these questions, yet they are essential to understanding how to sell anything to anyone. Here they are:

- How is this issue impacting your ability to enjoy life?
- How is this issue impacting other people?
- What might happen if you don't take action?
- What might occur if you *do* take action?

- Who else might need to be involved in your decision?
- If we can find the right solution for you today, how soon would you be able to start? Are you in a position to proceed? If not, why not?

What you're trying to do in this step is highlight how your services can benefit your client, as well as uncover any hidden objections that might make the difference between their seeking better health and suffering in silence. People who have learned to live with a health problem can be blind to the bigger implications and impacts of it, and part of your job is to gently coax them out of the shadows and into the light.

4. Enroll

The final step is to enroll the person to become a new patient or client. This should be the *first* time you offer a solution. This takes practice! Most of us race to the solution much earlier. (If you're not happy with your conversion rate, this could be why.) *How* you offer your solution is important. You just got done learning about the specific problems and issues that your prospect is having. This is not the time to give a canned speech about your services, your credentials, or anything else. Now is the time to match what you offer specifically to the outcome they want. If they're dealing with a thyroid issue, for example, trying to sell them an overall lifestyle program that includes everything from dietary protocols to stool testing is a surefire way to lose them. Focus on selling them the one thing they want right now. Once they agree to work with you and develop trust in you, there will be plenty of opportunity to discuss bigger programs and more services if they make sense down the road.

Here's how to enroll someone to become a new patient. Note

that each step follows logically from the previous step:

1. Listen carefully to what they tell you they want and repeat it back to them. Use the exact words they used to describe the issue. Be careful not to distort what they said, or they'll think you haven't been listening or are just trying to sell them something. If they say, "I'm really afraid of what's happening to me," say back to them, "I'm sorry to hear about your fear. Can you tell me more?"

2. Verify that they agree that what you said matches what they want. Then explain how your service specifically delivers the outcome they want. You might say something like, "Sharon, you said that you wanted some ideas on how to feed your kids healthy snacks after school that won't ruin their dinner. Is that correct?" [Verify.] "Well, one of the handouts I give my clients is a whole list of ideas along with recipes and even a grocery list to make it easy to shop for everything. Would you find that useful?"

3. They might agree to purchase your services on the spot, which is wonderful. Or they might ask questions or offer objections. Demonstrate that you understand their concern by using my suggestions on "Handling Sales Resistance" below.

4. After removing objections, again offer your targeted solution, incorporating the *exact phrases and desires* they stated during your meeting.

5. Address any additional areas of resistance. Always respond to an objection and then be quiet. Do not babble on. Wait for them to respond.

6. Ask if they have any further questions. Give them every op-

portunity to understand exactly what's being offered. Never talk a prospect into a sale. They will invariably go home and regret their decision and bail out. You want motivated clients who have a positive attitude toward you and cannot wait to get started with your services.

Handling Sales Resistance

You can prepare for this conversation as much as you like, but there will always be some resistance that you'll have to face. That's okay; people worry. They worry if they're making a good decision. They worry about losing face if they make a bad one. They worry about making a financial commitment. They worry about not being successful. They worry about whether they've chosen the right solution. The core of selling is educating and serving the needs of others, and education is the best solution for sales resistance. Your job is to guide them through their fears and worries, which are usually cost, impatience, change, and trust.

Here are my top responses for handling sales resistance when you encounter it. You'll probably come up with some of your own, but these are a good starting place:

How to Respond to Cost/Price Resistance

- Ask if they've done research on other solutions and their costs so you can determine their level of understanding of the value of your service. They might be comparing apples to oranges, making price irrelevant as a determining factor. You'll want to point this out.
- Review your services compared to others, and how you're

different from them. Do others offer ongoing email support? What about automatic ordering or discounts on dietary supplements? Do you use a unique protocol or method that you can highlight?

- Describe the options for making it affordable to work with you. Perhaps they can get started with a group program instead.

- Ask them what not fixing the problem is costing them, their family, and their quality of life. This is a big one! There is an emotional cost for those who struggle with a miserable quality of life that has no dollar value: pain and suffering. And it's likely the largest cost of all.

- Advise them about what their problem might cost long term if they do not handle the issue today. What might it cost down the road if they don't fix their blood sugar problem now? Don't manipulate them but point out that a problem like that can lead to surgery, vision issues, and nerve damage.

- Let them know that you offer payment plans to make your services more affordable.

- Tell them ways in which you served others and ask them which of those strategies might work for them.

How to Respond to Impatience and Issues of Change and Trust

- Ask if the very act of discussing their problem with you is making them feel any better. Have them acknowledge out loud how sharing with you has helped them feel more comfortable with you.

- Let them know that it probably took years for their problem to develop, so it will take some time to heal, too. This is how you differ from the allopathic medical model! Explain why the holistic model gets results versus masking symptoms.

- Remind them that big results can only come about through big changes, and that you will be there to guide them on their journey to better health. People don't like change, do they? But if they know you will be there to support them through the process, it might alleviate this deep-seated fear.

- Offer them your guarantee of services. A money-back guarantee isn't always possible, of course, so establish creative ways to minimize the risk of moving forward with you.

- Ask them what's stopping them from moving forward and address that issue head on. You might have a good idea about what's stopping them, but you don't know for certain unless they tell you. *Avoid assumptions and get the facts.*

- Ask them what they think will happen if they make no changes or decisions at all. Let them list all the possible downsides of *not* moving forward with you. Sure, you can tell them, but if they come up with their own list you can bet it will include things you haven't thought of. And, of course, it will become much more personal to them.

- Ask, "If you can achieve _____ [ideal outcome they have identified], would making some small changes in your diet or lifestyle over the next few months be worth your time and effort?" We know that doing the same thing over and over again and expecting a different result is futile; improvement requires change. Help them understand how the change will impact their life and give them exactly what they told you they want.

If the client is engaging with you, it means they're interested. Objections are simply an opportunity for you to provide gentle reassurance, which is what many people need. Just remember to smile and *be quiet* after you respond. Listen to what your prospect has to say.

Sales Don'ts

There are several things you should never do in the *Enroll* step of the PACE Sales Method. Here's a quick rundown:

- Don't speak over your prospective client's head. Meet them where they are, and avoid confusing medical-speak. They won't be compelled to take action simply because of your extensive knowledge of health or impressive vocabulary. Being present with them and conscious of their pain is the fastest way to gain their trust and commitment.
- Don't disparage the competition. That can only come back to haunt you later! Ours is a small community, and we all do better when we support each other. I've always believed that a rising tide lifts all boats. In a community that is too often attacked from outside, we need to have each other's backs.
- Don't dominate or interrupt a prospect who is pouring their heart out to you. They're in a fragile place and giving you the opportunity to safeguard their trust. If you steamroll them you'll both lose out on the opportunity to work together.
- Don't assume anything. You don't know what the other per-

son is going through until they tell you.

If the two of you are mismatched, or if the resistance just seems too strong, let them go. If they aren't saying, "Hell yes," then it's "No." Don't take it personally. "No" might simply mean "Not now." It might also mean "Not ever." That's okay! Unfortunately there are plenty of people out there who are unwell and need your help. Choose to work with only those who are fully on board and are committed to the process.

You might encounter a prospect who wants your attention for some reason other than getting well. Some people just want to chat because they're lonely! Others are narcissistic and expect you to listen to them talk about themselves for hours, but they never intend to pay you a nickel for your time. Remember, you are on a rock by the raging ocean, and it's your job to throw a life preserver to someone who desperately needs it. If you're getting nowhere with a prospect, gently say, "Why don't you go home and think about it? When you're ready for me, I'll be here. Thank you for coming to see me." And then lead them to the door. There are plenty of others hanging on for dear life in the swirling sea who need your attention right now.

How to Stop Giving Free Advice

Just a couple of the challenges you face are acceptance of your work by conventional thinkers and learning basic practice-development skills. Yet one of the trickiest of them all involves something much closer to home. Perhaps the following sounds familiar:

A well-meaning friend is struggling with her health and asks for your help. She promises, "I'll only need a few minutes of your time." But you know what she probably wants is free advice. My friends often want me to give them strategies for growing their businesses. In fact, just last week a practitioner friend of mine ended our personal conversation with "By the way, I really want to pick your brain on how to get more clients."

I'm always flattered at first... and want to help. But after the euphoria fades I feel more than a little peeved. After all, I make my living providing this service. Asking me to give away my intellectual property is no different from asking a friend who owns a clothing store to give you a free dress!

Here's the deal: all this free advice you're handing out? It harms more than it helps.

Free Advice Yields Lousy Results

Your ability to help people has tremendous value. In most societies, exchanging cash or a valuable asset for another valuable asset (product or service) is based on the rule of reciprocity; it's foundational to how nearly all societies have evolved.

A person who commits money in exchange for your help is communicating that they're serious about you and your work. It strengthens their motivation to make changes and stay compliant with your recommendations. So not only does collecting a fee for your advice help you financially, it increases the chances of a successful engagement.

Offering free health advice to friends typically delivers lousy results. They're not accountable for anything to anyone and have no vested interest in changing their behavior. Reciprocity is absent; the value exchange never takes place; you're out time, money, and energy; and your friend doesn't improve.

Unfortunately once you start giving your services away, it becomes harder to say no. This crumbling personal boundary steals not just from your wallet, but from your self-esteem. You may think that what you're doing is noble, but over time the only race you're winning is the one toward frustration. All those fifteen-minute sessions (which usually last an hour) add up, and it's exhausting to give away energy and time in the absence of results, joy, and money. So let's go through the fix for this.

My Method to (Gently) Say No to Freebies

When a friend asks me for a few marketing tips or to pick my brain on a direction for their practice, here's my response:

> "Hey, I'm happy to help. Let's set up a quick fifteen-minute chat to find out what's going on and then I'll let you know what I think it will take to get you back on track."

Four rules to adhere to with this approach:

1. Avoid helping them right then and there! You want them to value your time. It also gives you breathing room to get out of a sticky situation and take control of the conversation when you do have your talk with them.

2. Make your chat a phone call and not an in-person discussion. It's tough to cut off a conversation in fifteen minutes' time when someone's sitting in front of you teary-eyed and begging for help.

3. Never offer solutions during the free fifteen-minute chat. That's why it's called a "quick chat" and not a consult. Control the call and remind them at the start that you only have fifteen minutes and will direct the conversation in order to get to the meat of the issue. This gives you permission to gently interrupt and redirect them. Otherwise they'll spend thirty minutes reviewing their entire life story and you'll get nowhere.

4. In your chat, ask general questions like what they've tried thus far, what worked and what didn't, and how committed they are to resolving the problem. If they push for solutions, push back. You can't help them yet anyway without a more thorough assessment (which is something they must pay for since it's your intellectual property).

While on your call, the goal is to determine what you think it will take to help them. Then at the very end let them know in what ways you can work together to get the results they seek *along with the associated fees you will charge them.*

If they say, "Geez, can't you just give me a couple of quick tips now?" you can confidently let them know that based on your conversation there's a lot more going on behind the scenes than they realize and you cannot provide guidance of any sort without a full assessment.

They might admit, "Well, I'm a little tight on money these days, I was hoping you could just help me out as a friend." Some options for responses are:

- I'm sorry to hear about your money issues. I do offer discounted sessions for low-income individuals; would you like to explore this with me?

- It would be unprofessional—and even a bit careless of me—to offer health solutions without understanding the root cause of your issues. Why don't we set up a one-time consultation together so we can ensure that whatever I recommend has the best possible chance of success? I think you will love the experience! And I'm happy to extend to my friends and family a discount of 20 percent, if that helps.

- I regularly donate ten hours of my time each month to the local women's shelter. All of my other work is fee-based. Sorry, I just don't have time for more free support right now.

- This is how I earn my living. It just isn't fair to me or to my family to give away my time and expertise. I've worked very hard and spent a lot of money to get here. I hope you understand.

The Harsh Truth

I'm still disappointed by friends who feel their relationship with me entitles them to freely access the knowledge and skill I have invested years and money acquiring. For over forty years I have volunteered hundreds of hours of time and energy to organizations and individuals of my choosing for causes I believe in. That's how I give back to my community. For my friends I offer love. And that, I believe, is a lot... and all they should expect from me.

If you're growing weary of requests for free advice, it's time to draw the line. Value your time so that others will, too. Put a premium on your expertise and charge what you're worth to everyone who asks for help.

I know this is not easy to do. It takes a lot of courage at first. But once you get the hang of it you'll find that it becomes quite natural. And you will feel *so* much better about yourself, too.

7. Advanced Step: Your Signature Platform

Creating a signature platform takes your practice to a whole new level of impact. Remember when I wrote about *noise* earlier in the book? Establishing your signature clinical platform is *a powerful way* to rise above the madness of the marketplace and establish yourself as a health-care authority. If politicians strive to set themselves apart through a unique platform, then you certainly should, too.

I call this an "advanced step" because if you have not yet identified your specific niche or defined the outcomes your services deliver, building a signature platform is irrelevant. Be sure to go through the other elements of the PEACE Process before tackling this tactic.

A signature platform is your foundational, branded theme that answers the question "How does what you do give me what I want?" There are three big benefits of an effective signature platform:

1. It solves the specific problem that your niche market struggles with.
2. It distinguishes you in a noisy market.
3. It streamlines your time, energy, and financial resources

through the delivery of a unique clinical program with a variety of levels, prices, and modalities.

Here are just a few examples of practitioners and their signature clinical platforms:

Dr. Keesha Ewers	Autoimmune conditions: Healing from the Inside Out
Dr. Tom O'Bryan	Gluten sensitivity and celiac platform
Dr. Daniel Amen	Brain health platform
Dr. Sara Gottfried	Hormone health
Dr. Deanna Minich	Colorful foods, colorful life!

There are many, many more—yet not nearly enough. That's because practitioners struggle with niching and focusing. But once you establish your niche and focus, creating your signature clinical platform is the next logical step you'll want to take.

Here's how a signature platform benefits not only you, but also your clients:

- It makes your work more efficient and effective. By focusing on one specialty area, you don't need to know everything about everything. You spend your limited time, energy, and money on only the knowledge, resources, and tools that provide your niche market with exactly the services they want most and are willing to pay for.

- It makes competition a moot point. Practitioners who try to be all things to all people become masters at nothing. They end up chasing after the same clients as every other practitioner. But your clients want a specialist—the expert for their condition. Establishing a focused platform lets you stand out as an authority and expert in one specialty area. Everyone benefits: your clients get what they want, you build expertise through a platform of excellence, and you no longer compete with all the other generalists in your community.

- It simplifies how you promote your services and attracts only your ideal clients, making marketing a lot easier and more cost-effective.

- Your signature clinical *program*—the primary offshoot of your overall platform—lets clients benefit from your services at a price and in a format that works for them. Instead of investing all your time, energy, and money promoting one-to-one clinical consults at an hourly rate, you can scale your specialty solution at various price points. Your prospects often want to know whether your services can help them without spending a lot of money. Success with less costly options demonstrates your value to them, and that might be just the nudge they need to step up to your higher-level services. This gives clients who aren't ready to spend a lot an opportunity to test out your services instead of looking for someone who offers what you do at a cheaper price. Program scalability lets clients make progress in the manner or method they prefer, too. In the pages that follow, I discuss these aspects of your signature program further.

- You can create multiple revenue streams. Let me say that in another way: You can generate income without relying exclusively on one-to-one clinical visits! One of the hardest parts of your work is the emotional and physical demands of meeting with clients day in and day out. There are only so many clients you can see in a day, and beyond that your only option to increase revenue is through increasing your rates, which can only go so far. Why not generate revenue through parlaying your knowledge into other deliverables? There are many options, and successful practitioners are doing it every day. This alone is reason enough to put this powerful method into play once you've nailed down the PEACE Process.

• You get to do the things that you love and do best. Do you love group coaching? Maybe you're interested in creating self-paced online programs? The possibilities are endless when you begin to focus time, energy, and money on a unique platform and program and offer it through a variety of learning methods.

Like everything else in your practice, your signature platform should flow out of your purpose. Once you've gone through the previous chapters' exercises on purpose and developing your niche, you should start to see what your signature platform might look like. It will be the framework that drives all your activities: your public talks, your unique service offerings, your books, your blog, your social media... everything! So it must speak to your heart and fire you up in a big way.

Creating a Signature Clinical Program: Your Platform Deliverable

The keystone of a signature platform is your personal, custom, branded service offering, or what I call your "signature clinical program." Many practitioners miss the target when creating a signature clinical program by forgetting that people buy *what they want*—not what they need, not what *you* think they need, and not what *you* want to sell them. Racing to create a program without considering whether or not your target audience *wants it* is a huge waste of time and energy.

If you've been working through the PEACE Process, you should be getting a handle on what your niche client wants, what has worked, and where they continue to struggle. Of course, nothing beats talking to your existing clients. Ask how working with you has changed their lives. From this knowledge you can outline a program that has the best chance for success once you launch it.

When starting out, develop a program that has no more than four components. For example, if you're working with middle-aged adults suffering from joint pain, your program might have these four components: diet, yoga, supplements, and meditation. If you're focusing on young women who are trying to lose weight, your program components might be diet, stress management, exercise, and sleep. Studies show that if you give a person too many changes to make, it overwhelms them and compliance and interest wanes. Starting with just four components makes it feel achievable and makes it easy for you to get something quickly built and launched.

Next think about the ways in which you might deliver your information to patients. The table below, "Teaching Methods," will give you some ideas. For example, in addition to your private consultations you might want to write an ebook, offer group coaching, or develop video lessons. And here's where those four components are key: Each chapter, class, and video mirrors one of the four components: your ebook will have four sections, your group coaching program will have four classes, or you will provide four videos if that's the route you take.

Teaching Methods

Read	Listen	Watch	Group	VIP
Books	Mp3 audio files	YouTube	Seminars, Workshops	Clinical packages
Ebooks	CDs	DVDs	Conferences	Teach others (e.g. through supplement-company or professional-association sponsorships)
Newsletters, Articles	Podcasts, Radio shows	Streaming broadcasts	Retreats	Certify others in your program
Manuals	Voice broadcasts	Webinars	Coaching, Group visits	Contract work to others
Transcripts	Teleseminars	Web videos	Boot camps	Paid speaking gigs

I recommend starting with three pricing levels, such as an ebook, a webinar series, and personal clinical visits. Too many levels can confuse a potential patient about where to start, and a confused mind will not take action. Three complete, distinct options at different price points makes it simple for them to choose. There is no one right combination of components and pricing levels for your signature clinical program, and that's great news for you! You can choose what you enjoy creating, what you're good at, and what your niche market wants.

I've outlined some commonly-used prices below. There's some wiggle room, and you should consider the following:

- **Your location:** Your prices should be consistent with what the market will bear in your part of the world.

- **Your clients:** Do you work with an affluent or a low-income niche market? Your prices should appeal to your target audience *and* deliver a profit.

- **Your competitors:** While your advice is invaluable, asking $47 for an ebook is unrealistic when compared to a paperback that costs half that. Align your prices with what other similar products and programs cost.

- **Your personal involvement:** The more you are personally involved in service delivery, the more you can charge. After all, your time is money! Your involvement in a group activity is less customized than what you offer in a private consultation, therefore your per-patient fee should be lower.

Here are some guidelines at the time of this printing:

0 – $197:	Ebooks; books; small, self-paced programs with limited bonuses and materials
$297 – $497:	Workshops; group activities; medium, self-paced programs with valuable bonuses and add-on services
$597 – $1,997:	VIP activities, multiday live seminars, comprehensive online programs that include personal time with you, corporate wellness programs
Over $2,000:	VIP activities that include testing, long-term continuity programs, speaking gigs, consulting with corporate clients

Choose a name for your program that's compelling, appealing, and lets your prospective patient know exactly what outcome they will get by purchasing it. If you've done your research—paying attention to your patients, Google Alerts, and LinkedIn Group conversations—you're off to a great start.

I've prepared a sample program for you to look at below. Note in particular the outcomes that this specific market is looking for and how I incorporated those outcomes into my program deliverables.

Program Name: Positive Pregnancy Program

Niche: I help women who are pregnant or trying to conceive learn the best possible strategies for experiencing a worry-free pregnancy and setting the stage for delivering a healthy, happy baby.

Outcomes: After going through my program, women will be able to implement exercise, stress-reduction, healthy-diet, and gentle detox strategies to positively benefit their growing baby and nourish themselves in the process.

Program Levels:

I: Ebook: 4 Ways to Ensure a Positive Pregnancy
$9.97
Book sections: exercise, stress management, healthy diet, creating a toxin-free environment

II: Full-Day Workshop
$297 per person/$347 per couple
Workshop sections: exercise, stress management, healthy diet, creating a toxin-free environment

III: Private Consultation
$2,997
12 individual sessions; includes free access to all above items
PLUS prenatal supplements; personal guidance on diet, exercise, and stress-reduction; and ways to create a toxin-free
environment

My program name is the "Positive Pregnancy Program." There are three levels from which a person can choose. If they just want a sample or a taste of what my program is all about, they can grab my ebook for $9.97. Those who want a more personal touch but are not ready to commit big money just yet can choose a day-long workshop for $297. They can move from level to level in no particular sequence as they choose. In this manner, anyone can get started with me depending on their interests, preferred style of learning, and financial situation. Plus I'm able to do an activity I adore: lead workshops! I've also set myself up to leverage my income beyond one-on-one clinical work.

Down the road I might create the "Positive Pregnancy Program Advanced Class" to help patients do deeper and more personal work. There are no rules here. With a signature clinical program, the sky is the limit.

Fine-Tuning Your Signature Clinical Program

It's rare that the first release of your signature program knocks it out of the park. At Microsoft we often joked that we shouldn't expect our software to be a hit until we launched version 3.0. That's because developers are typically in their own heads during the creation phase without a lot of live testing in the real world. Unless you've been able to release your program to throngs of people prior to launch, you should probably expect to be a tad underwhelmed at your initial results. Don't sweat it. Understand that's par for the course and then move onward and upward toward improving it.

In fact, when I'm told by practitioners that they've tried the signature program idea but failed at it, I usually discover that the fine-tuning of the program was lacking. They had poor results from version 1.0 and assumed nobody wanted or liked what was delivered. Don't let that be your experience. Remember there should be at least versions 2.0 and 3.0 for fine-tuning what you've created to make it better, richer, and more valuable. Persistence is your best buddy here.

The Six-Step Method for Developing a Signature Program

Here are the six steps you'll need to go through to create your signature program. They're simple, but they take some work. Get started today and be ready to launch next quarter!

1. **Identify your target client's problem, desires, or needs.** By now you should have a pretty good idea of what those are by talking to past clients and by paying attention to Google Alerts, LinkedIn Groups, and any place your prospective client hangs out.

2. **Research solutions offered by your competitors.** What do they offer? What benefits are they promising? What are their pricing structures? What methods are they using to deliver their programs? Sleuth out what's already being offered to your target client for ways to create and differenti-

ate your program accordingly.

3. **Outline your program concept.** Look at the sample above that shows different kinds of learning methods and pricing structures. Determine what components you will include at various levels: self-paced content, one-on-one clinical work, supplements, group visits, online coaching, etc. Start with three levels and three price points, for example:

- Level 1 – Ebook with four sections devoted to the four components ($9.97)
- Level 2 – Group coaching program, four classes devoted to each of the four components, handouts and worksheets, supplements, and online forum ($297)
- Level 3 – VIP program, four individual clinical sessions devoted to the four components. Possibly include all components of levels 1 and 2, plus lab testing ($1,997)

4. **Build your program.** Devise the content and framework for each of the four components. If you offer self-paced or downloadable material, this is the step where you'll do your writing, recording, filming, and so forth. This will take some time. You might need to hire (or enlist) help to review everything for clarity, grammar, and even visual appeal. For example, ebooks and other material should include plenty of graphics as these help tremendously with engagement and learning. Things like spelling errors can turn off clients and prospects, so don't overlook the small stuff. Ask your friends and family members to proofread your text, or hire a freelancer to help.

5. **Release and promote your program.** Once you're done creating, release your signature clinical program to the world! Put it out there. Start telling people about it. Get feedback on it. Here are some promotional ideas:

   - Update your opt-in on your website to reflect your signature program.
   - Brand your social media pages and posts with your new signature expertise.
   - Schedule public talks to establish your expertise for your new signature program.
   - Come up with a fun logo for your program! Search locally or online for freelancers who can help you with this and meet your budget requirements.
   - Launch your program with an email or direct-mail marketing campaign.
   - Promote a webinar that outlines the four components of your solution and offer a special deal on one of the levels to get people enrolled.

   If you aren't 100 percent comfortable with broadly announcing your program, present it to a closed group first—friends, family, and people you trust to give you honest and open feedback. Offer it to them for a significantly reduced fee in exchange for their testimonials. That way you can start collecting endorsements for promoting the program later on.

6. **The reporting dashboard:** Evaluate your results and modify for your next version release. The reporting dashboard is a critical step that many fail to take. Review your early results to determine whether version 1.0 was a success

or needs some work. Is anyone buying it? What's your return on investment (ROI)? How about using Google Analytics to determine if people are staying on the program page of your website? What percentage of visitors to your program page is actually buying? Keep track of those who sign up and have clinical success, and which program level has the best rate of clinical success—that's a metric that definitely bears tracking!

If you don't hit your ideal metrics, run the program back through the six steps above. Maybe your content isn't quite there, or you don't have it priced right. Perhaps you need to do a better job of marketing the program. Before you pull the plug on what could be the basis of an awesome program, ask your circle of family, clients, and friends what's missing. Is it priced right? Is it compelling? Have you overlooked anything? Plug their feedback back into the development cycle and get ready to launch version 2.0!

Most of all, remember the immortal words of Commander Jason Nesmith in *Galaxy Quest*: "Never give up! Never surrender!"

Questions about Developing Your Signature Platform

When I talk about signature platforms in my live workshops, I'm often asked several questions that I'm guessing you might have, too. So let's go through those right now.

Q: Isn't this just for the rich and famous?

A: Nope, not at all. In fact, many of the rich and famous got to be rich and famous by getting crystal clear about their passions and their ideal target audiences, and then creating the platforms (and accompanying programs) to deliver exactly what their patients wanted! Most practitioners should take this approach to differentiate themselves and become the experts in their specific areas. This is especially true if your goal is to thrive, regardless of whether or not you care at all about becoming famous.

Q: Aren't others doing the same platform that I am?

A: If your focus is on any one of a number of prevalent conditions these days, then yes, certainly there are others using that platform. *But no one is doing it just like you.* Your protocol, method of delivery, style of delivery, brand, geography, and target audience differ. No one else can be you, or do what you do, except you. There are more sick people than there are people to take care of them, so unless you are getting too narrow in your program, there are plenty of clients to go around.

Q: I'm afraid of getting locked in to one specific platform. Can I ever change it?

A: Absolutely! The goal is to start with one thing—something, anything—and get really, really good at it. Learn everything you can about the condition; the market niche; clients' desires; and the protocols, supplements, and diets, and develop your method and your signature program that solves the problem. Once you've established your platform of authority you can evolve to the next platform. Want proof that it can be done? Just check out Dr. Mark Hyman's approach. After his wildly successful Blood Sugar Solution platform, he created his Detox platform. You can do the same thing, too.

Q: What about competition? How can I compete with other people who do what I do?

A: I don't believe that holistic health is a zero-sum game in which your gains must be offset by another's losses. If everyone selects a unique niche and develops their own signature program, we move from being competitors to being collaborators. You can create the biggest referral network in the world by being unique and distinct. We need to make holistic health a household term; we can't do that if some of us win and some of us lose.

Q: This sounds like a lot of work. How can I find the time to build something like this? I'm just so busy.

A: Building your platform does take some time and effort. And perhaps a little bit of money, too. But if your goal was to do something easy, you never would have chosen this path, would you? I contend that if you cut out all the tasks that are not likely to bring in business, eliminate the distractions that lead you nowhere, focus on a specific niche market, and carve out four hours a week to pull your ideas together, within a few months you'll be ready to go. It cannot happen without that kind of laser focus. So if you're tired of doing the same thing over and over again and not seeing results, and want to take your practice up to the next level of success, put in this effort. It will deliver returns, I promise.

8. Advanced Step: Messaging Mastery and SEO

Messaging is foundational to nearly everything in your practice. It's the biggest speed bump many practitioners encounter when setting out to build a website, create a signature talk, or do a social media posting. If you're stuck when it comes to creating patient-attraction messages, this chapter is for you.

The Patient-Attraction Messaging Framework

Your unique and distinct position in the market is tied to the messages you create. Developing messages involves integrating three key elements: your niche, your brand, and your promise. We've already gone through how to pinpoint the niche market you wish to serve. Let's now look at the other two messaging elements: your brand and your promise.

The Essence of Your Brand

Branding is a largely misunderstood piece of the pie, and it's vital to establishing your position as a trusted authority. You might think your brand is about your logo, the colors on your website, or the advertising materials you produce. It's not.

It's about how *others describe you.*

While your niche is all about whom you serve and the outcome they receive from working with you, your brand is about how you show up in the world. This is an important distinction. If you asked your best patients to describe you, what would they say? That's the question you want to answer in solidifying your brand. It's a question to pose to your family and the people in your life who know you and the services you provide. What are your ethics? What are your beliefs and opinions? What is your style, your character?

You are the most unique aspect of your practice, period. Your personal distinction sets the stage for establishing your brand in the market. There's no one else like you out there. And when you understand the power of Brand You, you are positioned to be the expert.

Many people have difficulty thinking of themselves as an expert; this is known as the *imposter syndrome.* (More about this in the following chapter.) Even the best of us have these thoughts. The great actress Meryl Streep once said, "Why would anyone want to see me again in a movie? And I don't know how to act anyway, so why am I doing this?"

The one thing no one can take away from you is who you are and what you're all about. There's no one who can do what you do because there's only one you.

One of the big bonuses when it comes to establishing your personal brand is that it seriously sidelines price-shopping on the part of potential clients. You're no longer a commodity. By creating Brand You, you reveal that you are different from everyone else, making your price less important. Different people do different things in different ways. Comparing you to someone else becomes meaningless.

By stepping into your distinctive brand, you make the first move in becoming the expert who claims a unique position in the market.

The Do-It-Yourself Branding Formula

Unless your goal is to become a household name or health celebrity, there's no need to invest big bucks in a consulting or public relations firm to help you develop your brand. The following do-it-yourself brand formula I borrowed from business leader Darren Hardy, the publisher of *Success* magazine, should work just fine. Your brand is:

- Who you are.
- What you do.
- Whom you serve.

That's just about it. For example, "I'm a holistic nutritionist and tireless health advisor for busy women suffering from chronic fatigue."

Here's my brand: "I'm a conscious and bold practice-building advocate and advisor for the holistic health community."

"Conscious and bold" is who I am. A "practice-building advocate and advisor" is what I do. The "holistic health community" is whom I serve. You might think this looks a lot like a niche formula, and there is a bit of overlap. While your niche formula is about how your specific clients receive the outcome they want, your brand is all about you. There *should* be some similarities here! You are looking for congruency in all aspects of your practice and the messages you put out to the community at large. So it all must synch up.

What I like about this three-part brand formula is its simplicity. It's great when you need a fifteen-second branding message. When somebody asks, "What's your byline?" you know what to say. Or if you want a simple signature line in an email or to put on your business card, you have those words ready to go. It's also great for the "about" section of your profile on social media.

Your Promise Is Paramount

Your promise is the commitment you make to your niche market, and it's another big part of your messaging. Obviously you can't guarantee that a specific clinical outcome will occur when a patient comes to you. But you can promise things that are in your control. You can guarantee that:

- You'll provide the highest quality client care possible.
- You'll work tirelessly to discover the root cause of their issue.
- You'll stay in touch with them regularly to make sure your therapy is working.
- They will never be left wondering what their action plan is.

You create your promise by filling in the blank in the following sentence: "If you work with me, I promise that _____ [is going to happen]."

Here's my example: "If you work with me, I promise that I'll help you discover and implement the simplest, most direct approach for achieving financial and personal freedom in your practice and in your life."

While you might not actually write your promise anywhere, it should be inscribed in your heart. When you speak to a client or prospect, you can explain exactly what you'll commit to doing for them, which sets their expectations from the start. It helps them feel comfortable about who you are and how you'll do your job. Clarity in your promise brings confidence to your prospects. And it could be the one key factor that many of your prospects use in deciding whether or not to work with you.

Messaging Magic

The intersection of your niche, brand, and promise form the sweet spot of what I call the "patient-attraction messaging framework." By developing marketing messages that integrate these three elements, you'll start to attract patients to your practice in a rational, focused way that lines up with who you are, whom you want to serve, and in what manner. The operative word here is *attract*; that's the goal, right? No one wants to hunt down new patients; we want them to find us. Being clear about these three elements of your messaging is your path to get there.

How do you take all of that stuff you've pulled together on niche, brand, and promise and create the right messages? To start, review the following examples of popular messages you're familiar with so you have a better idea of what I mean:

"The milk chocolate melts in your mouth, not in your hand." (M&Ms)

"When it absolutely, positively has to be there overnight." (FedEx)

"Fresh hot pizza delivered to your door in under 30 minutes... or it's free. Guaranteed." (Domino's Pizza)

Each of these marketing messages combine niche, brand, and promise without hitting you over the head with the specifics. Domino's Pizza is considered the classic in perfecting their marketing message. The minute you see it, you know exactly who it represents and what they're all about. Let's go through those three components—niche, brand, and promise—in the Domino's example.

The niche market is anybody who wants a pizza in under thirty minutes. Who might that be? The busy mom bouncing the kids between school and soccer practice. A bunch of guys sitting around watching *Monday Night Football*. The niche market is people who want their pizza fast and don't want to leave home to get it. "Thirty minutes, man. Gotta have it *now*."

The brand is fresh, hot pizza. As simple as that.

The promise is that you'll get it in "under 30 minutes or it's free. Guaranteed."

But what's missing from the Domino's equation? What do they *not* claim in their marketing message? If you thought *quality*, you're right. Few consider Domino's to be the premium-quality pizza on the market. But they don't even hint at that. And frankly their niche market doesn't care that much because that's not why they choose Domino's. *Domino's isn't trying to be all things to all people.*

What Domino's did is create a simple statement that set up their position in the marketplace without a lot of complicated mumbo jumbo. Their customers know exactly what they can expect from them. This is exactly what I'm encouraging you to do, too.

Sample Marketing Messages

I've developed dozens of marketing messages for my own business, and I want you to do the same. The goal of developing these messages isn't to publicly post them verbatim but to incorporate elements of your messages wherever you promote your practice. Writing them out is simply a way to help you formulate the words and plant them in your brain and in the brains of others. When people ask who you are and what you do, instead of grasping for the right words, rambling on about your services, or, worse yet, unloading a million ways that you work with people, your carefully crafted words will drop like jewels out of your mouth. When it comes time to create a talk for an upcoming conference you'll be able to submit your proposal along with one of your marketing messages to succinctly state who you are. When it comes time to update your website copy, your messages will guide the words you choose.

Here are the elements of your marketing messages:
- What you do
- What you believe
- Whom you serve
- How they will benefit
- How you serve them
- What you promise to them

Here are a few of mine:

"I am an expert at helping holistic health practitioners and companies have greater success so they can heal more people in an increasingly sick world."

"I believe that the holistic health community has an obligation to broadly promote their services in order to make holistic care a household term."

"I combine traditional marketing and cutting-edge digital strategies in my work with select clients who are bold, determined, creative, and have the courage to stand out among the competition and build the businesses of their dreams."

One of the goals of this third message is to intentionally alienate specific people. I'm very selective about who I work with. I push people to step up. I ask them to take chances. My clients must commit to focusing on a niche to work with. I only want to work with people who aren't afraid of doing the work and taking a few risks. People who do not fit that profile can work with someone who won't make those demands. In fact, I'd prefer it. Otherwise it will be a painful experience for both of us. You should do the same. In fact, I'll bet you have clients who should be fired... you know, the ones who cause you most of the heartache, drain your energy, and contribute the least financial return.

Strong messaging can do your work for you before clients even step foot in the door.

Exercise: Develop Three Marketing Messages

I encourage you to develop at least three marketing messages using your niche, brand, and promise as your foundation. Here are examples of marketing messages from someone in the holistic health community that you can model:

"I am an expert at helping families with young children have less illness and more energy so their kids can do better in school and sports and grow up to be amazing adults!"

"I believe parents have an obligation to help their kids thrive and must create a healthy environment so their kids can have the best chance for personal success as they grow up."

"Using evidence-based natural medicine in my work, I choose to enable families willing to make healthy lifestyle changes in order to build firm foundations for long-term health."

Keep in mind that your messages will evolve. As time goes on you'll write new ones as you get more clarity. Clients who come to see you will trigger more ideas. You'll have moments when you realize, "Oh, that's a great word. I'm going to use that word in my marketing messages."

The bottom line is this: Your messages should elicit an "I need your help" or "That's for me!" response from your future clients. That's when you know you've knocked it out of the park. This is the goal of all the marketing activities you take on, from the talks you give to the literature you put on your website and in your social media... everywhere. You want people to show up and say, "She's speaking to me; she knows exactly what I need. That's the person I want to work with."

Next time you're at a party and somebody asks, "Who are you? What do you do?" you can test out your messaging, gauge how people respond, and modify accordingly. Once you feel you have it nailed down, begin to incorporate the essence of your messages everywhere you have the opportunity to attract new clients.

There is no right or wrong when it comes to crafting your marketing messages, but craft them you must! Without this kind of clear and consistent articulation of your position in the market, you risk invisibility in a world that competes more and more for your prospective client's attention.

The Nuts and Bolts of SEO

Search engine optimization, or SEO, is likely the most confusing aspect of attracting prospective clients online, and this section provides only a general, big-picture idea of what *search marketing* is. I encourage you to do some research on your own on this topic and to make sure you have a general idea of the importance of SEO as it relates to messaging.

Search marketing allows you to get the best results from your online assets—website, videos, blogs, etc.—by boosting your website's traffic and building trust with your audience once they arrive. There are two sides of SEO to ensure this happens: a technical side and a content side. An "optimized" website is one that has considered both sides of this equation; when both are set up effectively, your links appear near the top of the results presented to a viewer when they run a search for your services. Of course, the goal isn't simply to optimize for search "traffic," it's to optimize for conversions; that is, when they click on a link and get to your website, they opt in to your email list, buy something from you, or get in touch for a consultation, for example.

Search engines such as Google and Bing are simply vast indexes of the internet. These systems read and categorize billions of webpages to help people find exactly what they're looking for when conducting a search. Each search engine has its own recipe, or *algorithm*, for turning all this information into useful search results. The search engine essentially reads and indexes the text on your website. Your goal is to make sure that when people are searching for the kind of help you provide, your website (or other online asset) ranks as high up in the search result as possible, preferably on page one or two. To do this, your website and other online media must have all the right ingredients for the search engine recipes.

The only side of search marketing I can speak to is the content side. For the techy stuff you'll want to enlist help from an SEO technician.

Algorithms change constantly, as they are based on artificial intelligence and are learning more each day, so be aware that the following information may change. However, as of this writing, here are the important *content* elements of search engine algorithms that you should pay attention to:

1. **A blog on your website.** I realize that you might cringe at the idea of writing an active blog on your website. However, from an SEO perspective, an active blog—even just one article per month—lets your visitors know that you have an active and lively business that is doing well. The content must be high-quality, niche-focused, and, if possible, generate inbound links from other sites or from other pages

on *your* site. Be sure to review my suggestions earlier in the book about how to get good at writing.

2. **Easy navigation.** Avoid focusing on pretty and/or complicated navigation tabs, and make getting around your website user-friendly, with logical, scannable text and clickable links corresponding to each page and section of your website. While your users prefer a simple, uncluttered, and visual (graphical) experience, Google prefers a simple, "crawlable" format that includes some written copy.

3. **Keywords, key phrases, etc.** Successful SEO on your website means that you have identified and used keywords and phrases that will attract prospective clients. These serve as a type of code that search engines use when someone performs a search on those terms. If there is a match between the terms a user searches for and one of your keywords or phrases, the greater the likelihood that the search engine will show it in the results for that user. The criteria for determining the best keywords and phrases are extensive, to say the least. The basic idea is to ensure that you're consistently and diligently integrating niche-specific keywords and phrases in all your online assets.

Algorithms, trends, and new ideas arise all the time, but the fundamentals of SEO remain, as always, to provide the best user experience possible in order to get high rankings in search engines. Provide targeted content that your ideal client seeks, and you'll increase your odds of achieving visibility through searches. As with all things marketing, let your clients' desires be your guide when it comes to SEO.

9. | **Fortifying a Power Practice**

In the preceding pages you've come a long way toward creating a practice that will thrive. I call that a "power practice." I hope I've been able to convey to you how important it is that you build a power practice that's healthy and profitable, not merely to enrich yourself—although there's nothing wrong with being fairly paid, but so you can better serve your clients and help them live happier, healthier lives.

Still, it often takes a mindset shift to secure a rock-solid power practice. The PEACE Process is a proven marketing method, but no method in the world can help you thrive unless you commit to working through the mental blocks you encounter.

Dealing with Fear, Uncertainty, and Doubt

In the five years since I published the first edition of *The PEACE Process*, I've identified a handful of concerns that are common obstacles to success. Each deserves discussion. I've listed them below along with some ways to deal with them.

"I'm not ready yet! There's still more stuff for me to finish."

Concern about not being "done" with everything, such as your website, setting up social media, finalizing your services, or wrapping up a class you're taking, stops many healers in their tracks. What starts out as "I just have to finish one more thing" often turns into a pause of many months, sometimes years! But getting everything done isn't critical because your niche will change, as will your practice model. So will your goals, your packages, your messaging, your website—all of it! This will happen as you meet with clients, new mentors, and peers, and as the dynamic of market conditions changes and new trends take hold. Stay open to change and avoid getting attached to things that might keep you stuck or scared to move forward.

Much of your work will never have a hard stop. The essence of entrepreneurship is accepting that flexibility is fundamental. You no longer have a boss, or regular performance reviews with clearly defined objectives and end dates, to direct your work; you are the captain of your own ship. The finish line will regularly move on you, whether you like it or not. The ability to shift and change, to stay agile and nimble, is, in my opinion, one of the most fun aspects of working solo. It might be different from what you're used to, and can be a little nerve-wracking at first, but I adore the freedom it provides, and you will, too.

Be mindful though. I'm not suggesting that you start a lot of things and then abandon them at your leisure! I'm encouraging you to accept the fact that, especially when you're new at this, you will often be faced with flying the plane while building it.

Chances are you're more ready than you realize, and ready enough to start. It's GO time!

Imposter Syndrome

In case you're unfamiliar with imposter syndrome, it's a psychological pattern in which a person doubts their accomplishments and has a persistent, internalized fear of being exposed as a fraud, even in the face of external evidence of their competence.

For example, you might be thinking, "Who am I to launch a practice? I'm just out of school and new at this." Or your doubts might be about being unable to help others with their health issues because you still haven't gotten your *own* issues resolved. I've heard friends say, "I don't *feel* like a nutritionist, I don't *look* like one, I still eat [name the guilty pleasure here]; how can I, in good conscience, help others?"

You don't know everything, and you're not perfect. However, you know more than your client—way more. You can best learn what you don't know by doing the work, not by sitting in your house reading another book about it and hoping that someday soon you'll be "ready."

My advice? *Get in the game and your self-confidence will skyrocket.*

Charging What You're Worth

Many of you practice in accordance with very clear licensing laws under which it's illegal to diagnose, treat, cure, prevent, or heal people from disease. Regardless of your credentials, the most important work you do is to guide and educate your clients. If you've ever worked with a coach, you know how *powerful* it is to simply have someone else's ear. In fact, the value of listening to your clients who've been ignored or poorly treated by conventional medical personnel for years is not only priceless, it's what they crave most.

If you don't believe me, do the research. Survey data shows that in medicine, technical proficiency is significantly less important to people than a *personal relationship with their provider*. In fact, research has shown that people who like their provider will not sue them even if they cause harm!

There's a (mis)perception in our industry that what we offer is so important, so vital that we should do it for free. To be honest, that makes absolutely no sense to me unless you have an oil well planted in your backyard and are doing this work as a hobby.

Doctors, lawyers, and plumbers don't give away their services... neither should you. Never underestimate your value. Undervaluing your services sends the wrong message to others.

Rethink your role as a guide who gives people hope for a better future. That's what they want from you. It's what you are qualified to do and what they are more than willing to pay you for. You deserve to earn a solid living helping them achieve exactly what they want.

Fear of Failure and Putting Yourself Out There

It's normal to feel frightened when stepping out over the ledge hoping that the safety net is there ready to catch you if you fall. In fact, few phobias are more widespread than the fear of failure when opening up shop.

I'd like you to once more dig deep and ask yourself what you fear most: to pursue your dream and potentially not make it; or to remain in a profession or job that you hate, spending your days angry and miserable, working toward building someone *else's* dream, and heading down the path toward a stress-related health condition? Any idea might fail; does it make sense to kill the one desire that you most yearn for because it *might* fail? Would you be able to live with yourself if you quit before you even start?

I don't have all the answers when it comes to dealing with this fear; I only know what has worked for me and for many others in our industry. The solution is to begin directing your energies outward versus living inside your head. Getting busy, taking one step at a time, and opening yourself up to the amazing opportunities that the universe wants to put in your lap can do wonders for battling and terminating those internal demons.

In a business course I co-created for the Nutritional Therapy Association (based on the PEACE Process method), this fear would crop up at first... and then as the class proceeded we noticed something magical happen. Students slowly began to talk to people in their regular day-to-day activities—in their book clubs, in their church groups—about their niche and the outcomes they helped others reach. These little baby steps outward began to attract opportunities that were least expected! All of a sudden a request to speak, or to partner, appeared from nowhere. If you're a believer in getting back what you put out into the world, you understand this already.

Don't discount the value of your energy, mindset, and positive attitude to tackle this beast and attract clients. The following well-known story describes this best.

An old Cherokee was teaching his grandson about life: "A fight is going on inside me," he said to the boy. "It is a terrible fight and it is between two wolves. One is evil—he has anger, envy, sorrow, regret, greed, arrogance, self-pity, guilt, resentment, inferiority, lies, false pride, superiority, and ego."

He continued, "The other is good—he is joy, peace, love, hope, serenity, humility, kindness, benevolence, empathy, generosity, truth, compassion, and faith. The same fight is going on inside you—and inside every other person, too."

The grandson thought about it for a minute and then asked his grandfather, "Which wolf will win?"

The old Cherokee simply replied, "The one you feed."

The days of filling your plate with fear, uncertainty, and doubt are over. Colin Powell once said, "There are no secrets to success. It is a result of preparation, hard work and learning from failure." Start failing so you can start succeeding. The world needs your help.

How Your Inner Critic May Be Stealing Your Dream

Are you managing your mental chatter, or is it managing you?

A few years ago my husband, Jay, and I took two weeks to bike from Prague to Vienna for our twenty-fifth anniversary. We traveled with twenty-one people whom we'd never met, and what I learned from this adventure, combined with a few related discoveries since then, was eye-opening.

The bike trip was advertised as "a hilly course with plenty of challenges." So Jay and I were perplexed and dismayed to hear repeated complaints from others in the group that the course was too hard. Only three of us did the long mileage each day.

At breakfast one day, one of the women told me that she was terrible at riding hills. So I challenged her with, "You can't get good at riding hills unless you actually *ride* the hills." And that day we rode the hills together. At the top of a very long and difficult climb through the forests of the Czech Republic, she was beaming! The next day we rode the hills together again. And the following day, too. Because what she had effectively done was rewire her brain into "I can" thinking as opposed to believing "No way can I do that."

Research shows that the average person talks to themselves about 50,000 times a day, mostly about themselves. And a full 80 percent of that self-talk is negative! For example, "I can't do hills." Or perhaps more like what I often hear: "I'm terrible at marketing," "I don't like selling," "It's impossible to be successful in this market," "People won't want to pay for my services," and "That will *never* work."

Why this is dangerous is that not only do these negative thoughts make you feel scared, frustrated, and paralyzed, but they become part of your makeup. Any neuroscientist will tell you that the more you think about something—especially if it has an emotional component to it—the more you reinforce the pathways connecting the neurons in your brain. The more you say these things to yourself, the more you believe them. Negative thinking starts its downward spiral, reinforcing our feelings of frustration, fear, and even victimhood.

In the book *Love Yourself like Your Life Depends on It,* author Kamal Ravikant describes how deeply loving yourself can crush the nasty habit of beating yourself up. Ravikant poses this question: "If I loved myself truly and deeply, would I let myself experience this?" In other words, would you allow anyone else talk to you the way you talk to yourself? If not, why are you doing it to yourself?

It's time to disrupt the negative playback loop and make friends with your inner critic!

Here's how it works: At the end of something positive—an amazing client consult, the delivery of a successful talk, or finishing your latest blog post—before you dash off to your next task, take a moment to let yourself feel good about your accomplishment. Simply take a few deeps breaths, genuinely congratulate yourself, smile, and let yourself feel the satisfaction of moving one step closer to your dream. That's all it takes.

When I finish a task I often walk into Jay's office and high-five him. This very simple practice takes only a few seconds and, in my experience, noticeably steps up my desire to get out and do more challenging tasks more often.

The positive effect of this small activity isn't immediate, because unlike negative emotions that have specific responses such as the fight or flight response, the effects of positive emotions are much broader in nature and slower to develop. It takes more time for these simple actions to work their magic and build the neural networks that connect you to a positive mindset.

Practice positivity. It will transform *everything* in your practice... and in your life.

Persistence Delivers a Power Practice

A power practice isn't built overnight. Persistence is essential to increasing your client base and, by extension, your sales and profits. Far too many fledgling practices fail because the practitioner didn't follow up often enough to produce results. A sale is rarely made after just one contact; most sales are made after the seventh or eighth contact. It's usually release 3.0 (to use my earlier software metaphor), meaning it takes multiple updates or versions of your services, website, or other business enhancements before you see success. In fact, it's commonly said that it can take anywhere from eighteen months to two years to make a new business fully functional and profitable.

Never give up; the winners are those who have staying power. Remember that your goal is to use your knowledge and skills to help people who are diseased, damaged, or distraught. It's a vulnerable and sensitive constituency, so allow time for them to accept you— *and for you to accept yourself.*

Referrals are a great way to generate new business. But don't just wait for former clients to refer others to you. Proactively ask for referrals from existing clients, allied health professionals, acquaintances, family, and friends. Send an email or snail-mail letter letting everyone know you are "open for business," sharing your niche focus, website URL, and even a coupon code for first-time clients. Don't assume they already know what you do and who you do it for! Most don't, and many aren't even familiar with the field of holistic health care. Remind them that you are taking new clients and you would love their support. Of course, always graciously thank someone who refers a new client to you.

Take a personal interest in your clients and prospects. Send them helpful articles you think would interest them. If you know of an event that your prospect or client will be celebrating, such as a birthday or anniversary, send them a card or a small gift. They will appreciate your thoughtfulness and remember you when they need your services or if they know someone else who does.

Marketing is a skill that's based on both knowledge and experience—and you can acquire both. One fast way to gain that knowledge is to find a mentor or to associate with someone who knows what works and has done it successfully. Talk to them about their experiences in generating new clients, references, and testimonials.

When crafting your marketing message, remember that you should never try to force people to purchase your product or service; find people who want your product or service, and focus on providing them with helpful information so they can make an informed decision.

How a Visual Roadmap Can Keep You Focused

Now that you've learned the basic concepts of how to market your services, you need a way to stay organized and focused. You've probably heard that every business needs a business plan, and the mere thought of creating a business plan may have you wanting to jump off a cliff. You might think that since you're a small business, perhaps a solo operation, you don't need a plan. That's just not true.

Regardless of size, every business must have a plan in place that is reviewed on a regular basis to guide its practice-building activities. There are no exceptions to this rule. You are responsible for the success and failure of your business, and if you don't know where you're going, you'll never get there.

The objective is to craft a marketing plan *that is connected to your purpose* so it can withstand distraction, interruption, lack of willpower, and inertia. Your connection to your purpose steers your plan; your plan engages your time, energy, and money.

Do you detest the thought of writing out pages and pages of text that you know you'll never look at again? I don't blame you; I won't do that either. I suggest that you create something a little different—a *visual roadmap* to guide your marketing strategies and decision-making. *Mind mapping* is not only a powerful and fun alternative to lengthy, text-heavy, conventional business plans, it suits your profession perfectly.

Your work is a combination of science and art. One key difference between you and the allopathic practitioner is that you not only rely on science and research, but also on the creative and intuitive elements of health and healing. That's what makes you great at getting results! The combination of science and art is the ideal holistic framework for delivering optimum health outcomes.

Mind mapping allows you to tap in to the logical and creative parts of your brain in a holistic manner to develop a marketing plan that reflects who you are, what you want to accomplish, and how you plan to do it.

While the term *mind mapping* was made popular by author and educational consultant Tony Buzan, it's an ancient practice. In the third century CE, the philosopher Porphyry of Tyros developed similar visual records in which he graphically visualized the concept categories of Aristotle. Philosopher Ramon Llull (1235–1315) used a similar approach. For our purposes I reference the ideas from Tony Buzan's website, and I strongly recommend that you check out one of his books—I use them faithfully.

Mind mapping works more effectively than a traditional, linear business-planning document in that it replicates the way your brain patterns and processes work. In real life we don't think in a straight line; we do not have one thought, and then a second thought, and then a third thought, and so on in a linear fashion. Our thoughts are more like a network. Our minds jump around from one thought to another thought (related or unrelated), and not necessarily in a sequential or linear manner.

To see some typical mind maps, simply do an internet search for "mind map" and choose "images." You'll see hundreds of them. Some are very simple while others look like tangled bowls of spaghetti. At the center of a typical mind map is the key topic or subject being mapped, such as your business. Lots of primary and then secondary branches of thought related to the key topic lead off from the center.

What's so great about the way this works is that while you're creating a branch, if you all of a sudden have a thought related to another branch you can instantly jump over and add to that branch without messing up what you were doing or losing your train of thought. Try doing that while creating a linear document!

As your ideas expand and new thinking evolves, you can build on your existing mind map simply by adding new branches.

Not only does this replicate the way your brain works, but over time it still makes perfect sense. I've gone back to mind maps I created twenty years ago and still relate easily to what I mapped out. It's fun, powerful, and painless.

Here are some helpful guidelines for creating your mind map. I adapted these from Tony Buzan's site:

1. Start in the center of a blank page turned sideways. This gives your brain freedom to spread out in all directions and express itself freely and naturally.

2. Use an image or picture for your central idea. An image is worth a thousand words and helps you use your imagination.

3. Use colors throughout, because colors are as exciting to your brain as are images.

4. Connect your main branches to the central image and connect your second- and third-level branches to the first and second levels, etc. Your brain works by association; it likes to link two (or three or four) things together. By connecting the branches you understand and remember the pathways easily.

5. Make your branches curved rather than exclusively straight lines, because straight lines are boring to the brain.

6. Label the branches as you go, using one key word per branch. Single-word labels give your mind map more power and flexibility.

7. Use images throughout. Because each image is worth a thousand words, if you have only ten images in your mind map, it's already the equivalent of ten thousand words of text.

As you review the PEACE Process to begin your marketing plan, create a mind map linked to your purpose. Review it prior to the start of each week, before you get busy, so you're crystal clear on what must be done that week toward building a practice that thrives right along with your clients. It's foundational to staying focused and moving forward in a world determined to pull you off center. Don't let it. Don't *ever* let it!

Time Investment

If you're like most holistic practitioners, you entered the profession not because you have an MBA, but because you want to help people be healthy and live longer. And that's good. But in order to do your job effectively and reach as many people as possible, you need a power practice. This requires a set of skills that work seamlessly together. Your clinical skill is important; I assume you have that in spades. And since you've read up to this point, you know how to market your business and bring in new clients who need your help. Now I'd like to talk about something that's not on everyone's list of exciting topics—time management.

For over twenty-five years I've been working with executives; athletes; and, most recently, holistic health-care practitioners, and the key difference between those who achieve success and make a big difference in their lives and in their work and those who don't is an unshakable commitment to setting boundaries regarding their time.

You'll note that I called this section "Time Investment" instead of "Time Management." We can't *manage* time. That's absurd, right? Many of us have read books or gone to seminars on time management, but we still don't have a grip on it.

I want you to think in terms of *time investment*. Not managing your time. Not spending your time. And heaven forbid, not wasting your time. Think about how you *invest* your time. When you invest your time, you expect to get a return—a *return on investment* (ROI). You expect to build your practice and you expect to help your patients live better lives. This means being selective about how you use your time.

A nutraceutical company once asked me to do a survey of their practitioners. One of the questions we asked them was "What's your biggest challenge in your practice?" And one of the top three answers was "I have too much to do."

We all have too much to do. I don't know anyone who walks around saying, "Hmmm, I have some extra time; I wish I knew what to do with it." The real issue is that we spend too much time on things that don't take us forward.

Most of us have more items on our task list than we can possibly imagine ever completing, and the majority of us are type-A perfectionists, adding *more* things to our task list every day! What's at the core of this issue is our *focus*. We spend too much time on activities that are not productive or not sufficiently enriching our lives.

For example, the average American spends thirteen years of their life watching television. Thirteen years! Somebody did a quick calculation on that and discovered that if you use an average of $250 a day in lost revenue in your adult earning years, those thirteen years account for over a million dollars gone. Just think about that for a minute. Too many of us make poor choices and let distractions control our focus.

No one should work twenty-four hours a day; we all need time to relax and regenerate. I have nothing against television, but when you watch TV, do it purposefully. Do it because there's something on that you want to watch. The important thing is to avoid wasting your time with mindless nonsense. How many cute kitten videos do humans *need* to watch? How much time does any person *need* to spend on Facebook? Does anyone *need* to play Candy Crush Saga?

It's a matter of acknowledging and honoring the value of your time. I could ask you, "Are you in control of your life?" But the real questions are: "Are you a hamster on a wheel, or the pilot of your life?" "Are you running around in circles and being controlled by everything else going on around you, or are you consciously engaged?" and "Are you in reactive or in proactive mode?"

The reactive person wakes up in the morning, grabs their smartphone, scrolls through their email, checks social media and news headlines, peeks at their calendar, and lets all these dictate their mood and schedule for that day: what they're going to do and, worse yet, what's irritating them. That's reaction.

The proactive person wakes up in the morning; possibly meditates, reviews their mind map, or does some journal writing; and thinks, "What must be done? What do I need to do to take me forward, to take me where I need to go?"

When you get up, do you say, "Oh, I gotta go to work today," or are you living your dream? There's a difference, and time investment is at the root of that difference.

The CPR Model of Performance Excellence

I've discovered that all the people with whom I've worked—regardless of what they did for a living and what their life was about, whether they were an athlete or a superstar in corporate America— have within them three key things that dictate performance excellence—*capabilities, resources,* and *purpose.* I call it the "CPR model," and it especially applies to holistic health professionals.

Let's start with capabilities. There are a boatload of things that you have to be good at and that impact your time. The demand for your capabilities is endless. You have to be great in your field and in the technical work you do. You have to know how to hire and fire. You have to be good at practice development and marketing your business. You have to plan and strategize. If you're writing a book, you have to know how to write. If you do speaking engagements, you have to be great at pulling together and presenting powerful talks. You have to stay current on all the latest research.

The resources you need to bring to bear to support that success are huge. You have to understand the technologies and the infrastructure to run your practice. Whom do you need to partner with? What kinds of people have to be on your team? Where do you invest? How much should you charge?

The driver that most time-management experts miss is your purpose. It's your big "why." If you don't understand what your "why" is and what your purpose is, how do you know what you should be studying or learning? How do you know with whom you should be partnering? Who to hire? Where to speak? Without that, it's like rearranging deck chairs on the Titanic. You're just doing work with no real purpose or no real end in mind. Time-management experts forget to teach us how to do that. They provide the tactics—you know, pick your A priorities and your B priorities—and that's great; but there's a transformation that has to happen first. If you don't get that purpose thing figured out then none of the other stuff will matter. You can manage all your agenda items perfectly, but you risk not accomplishing your big goals.

Choose instead to *invest* your time more effectively so you can serve more patients, build the practice of your dreams, and live the life you desire.

Let's dispel some myths, especially ones about how we invest our time. Myths and truths in our heads are beliefs that dictate how we feel, which impacts our behaviors, which give us our results.

Top Truths about Time

Without further ado, here are my top ten truths about time—in reverse order:

10. What *you* think doesn't matter half as much as what your *client* thinks. It's better to invest your time with them listening than talking.

9. If you fail to plan, you are planning to fail. Develop a game plan, business plan, or mind map so you can focus your time on the things that lead you to meeting your goals.

8. Desire without method is nothing more than hope. If you've wanted to get better at time investment, but you haven't implemented a method for doing it, you're living in hope. And guess what? Hope doesn't pay the bills. Live

your desires!

7. C priorities can be just as important as A priorities. Remember that ficus tree that gnawed at my peace of mind day after day until I took care of it? Taking care of that C priority recharged my willpower battery and was every bit as important as tackling the big task in front of me. Do these too... just don't make them your primary focus.

6. To-do lists are no guarantee that the listed tasks will ever get done. How many people have a to-do list? How many people have *seven* of them, like me? People with type-A personalities say, "I have to do *this* and I have to do *that* and I have to do the other thing"—that doesn't mean anything is moving forward. Your mind map is more effective for time investment than all your to-do lists.

5. We don't have more to do today than ever before—we've just lost our focus. During most of the last century when most people had industrial and manufacturing jobs, they had only so many things to get done by the end of the day. They'd build so many widgets or account for so many pennies. When they returned home, they were done. But now it seems our work is never done. How about that book you want to write? What about those client issues you have to research at night? And because you're never done, you never stop. You're always busy, and that means you have less brainpower to do the important needle-moving tasks. You have to focus on those tasks to get where you want to go.

4. By giving people *more* of your time, you often serve them

less. Many of us enter the holistic professions believing we have to give and give. Sometimes it's because we're trying to make up for all the bad advice that our clients have had to deal with up to this point. As a result you end up over-giving and spending more time with clients than you should. Invariably somebody suffers down the road. It might be the next person who's supposed to come in after that client, your office staff who must deal with unhappy clients in your reception area, or your family who is waiting for you (again) for dinner; but you suffer the most. Give your clients more *quality* time, not more time.

3. Your schedules don't need to be managed... your boundaries do.

2. People don't steal your time; you hand it to them. I call this point, and number three above, my "victim points." Going through life thinking that your time is being stolen from you is victim mentality. Your time is your own responsibility. It's the most valuable, precious commodity you have. Once it's gone, it's gone forever. Accommodating constant and random interruptions communicates to others that their time is way more valuable than yours. Don't hand your time over to someone else unless it's the best use of your time.

1. You don't *have* time... you *make* time. For example, it seems everyone thinks about writing a book (and should!). I've written two books now, and it's an amazing process to go through. I talk with many practitioners about the books they're writing. I might say to them, "So how are you com-

ing on chapter seven?" "Well, I was going to work on that, but I didn't have time this week." But they're just choosing to do other things. Whether you've chosen to write a book, paint your office, take an evening course, or get another degree, you are the final arbiter of your time. Choose what's important to you and let the other stuff go. No one can do it all!

Here's How "Why" Impacts Time

When you get to "why," everything clicks into place. If someone says to me, "I want you to come do a marketing talk for a group of accountants," even though I *could* do that, I think to myself, "Why *would* I do that?" If someone wants me to do something that pulls me off center or away from my ultimate goal—which is to take natural health and integrated health care as wide and as far as possible—I would refuse that request. Why would I spend my precious time and energy on anything outside of my "why"—my purpose?

It's amazing what happens when you guard your time this way. All that you do magically becomes relevant. I don't do anything that isn't in line with my purpose anymore. I can say no. I know my boundaries and I do it guilt-free because I have a bigger mission. While practicing nutrition I realized that I could have a bigger impact by blending my skill in the area of sales and marketing with my desire to help people heal naturally. So I switched gears in order to help practitioners get their messages right. And that is what my "why" is all about.

There's one great benefit to honoring your "why." Remember the Simon Sinek quote in chapter 2? "People don't buy *what* you do. They buy *why* you do it." This is powerful information. Sinek explains that when you get connected to your "why," your clients want to work with you because you're working in congruence with who you are and what you're about. You start to exude a certain level of confidence that attracts them to you like crazy!

Getting connected to your "why" allows you to effectively manage your time and your boundaries. What you believe and what you think impact your results, and your beliefs and thoughts come from your "why." It's another part of the mindset shift needed to get results. If you believe it's okay for others to steal your time and invade your boundaries and dictate your agenda, you're going to start feeling resentful and frustrated. And if you let it happen, you're not going to get anything done. That impacts your results. Conversely, if you believe it's up to you to set your boundaries and agenda, and you integrate your feelings with that, you'll begin to see extraordinary results.

What Can You Fix Today?

I've talked about transformation—the things that have to happen from a "why" mindset in order to make progress. Now let's get tactical. Below are some practical tips that can double your results. They're not hard—they're changes. Take one at a time; don't do them all. I'm sure they'll bear fruit.

- **Fifty-Minute Time Blocks Using a Productivity Timer**
  I love blocking time. This has become my most powerful business tool. It works best when you're tackling difficult projects or tasks. Using a timer, block out fifty minutes of your time, three times a week. Let's say you're writing a book. You decide, "I'm going to write my introduction this week." Set the timer for fifty minutes. Don't take phone

calls. No checking email. Shut the door. Let nothing short of an emergency interrupt you. Work on one thing and one thing only for fifty minutes. When the timer goes off, stop, get up, get some water, walk around, and return to a new task; do this to recharge your willpower battery.

- **One-Touch Process for Email**

Too many people have emails sitting in their inbox that have been there for weeks or months. They see the same emails day after day thinking, "Oh, yeah, I have to do something with that."

Here's your new email process: touch it once, do something with it, and never touch it again. You either file it away for future reference or act on it by replying or responding the first time you read it. This is important: The first time you read it, do something with it. Act on it. Delegate it. Forward it to somebody else who should deal with it. Eliminate it; that's what the delete button is for. Reschedule it, because of course there are some things you simply can't work on right now. Prepare a folder that says "Monday" or "the 30th," put it in there, and on that day put a time block together and work on it. But don't just let it sit in your inbox.

You get extra points for unsubscribing to all those random newsletters you keep getting that you never read. Have you ever started reading a newsletter and then began linking out to a billion other places? Yeah, me too. Before you know it, thirty minutes are gone and you've done absolutely nothing to move forward.

- **Replenish Willpower Glycogen – Two Hard Tasks for Each Simple One**

  Replenish that "willpower glycogen" we talked about earlier by taking on one mundane task for every two hard ones. Simple. It's especially useful and therapeutic to take action on some issue or irritant that you've been tolerating. That kitchen drawer that needs to be cleaned out? The dispensary that needs to be organized? Do something that doesn't take the kind of brain power that the harder tasks do. It's amazing how great it feels to not only get something done that's been bugging you but to replenish your willpower at the same time. And you effectively get back to a harder or more meaningful task more productively later on.

- **Take Three Days Unplugged Every Three Months**

  For you workaholics and digital dependents, here's the scary one: Take three days unplugged every three months. You can do it at home or you can make it a special event. I once went to Hawaii with my husband to watch him compete in the Ironman World Championship. After it was over we decided we were going to unplug for four days. No electronic anything! We were only allowed to check for urgent voicemail messages. Otherwise no PC, no phone, no nothing, totally off. And it was hard. I kept looking for the dopamine hit.

  It's become typical behavior to sit on the beach taking pictures and posting them on social media. You merrily upload as you say, "I have to show people this beach I'm on!" And you post the photos of the beach and your friends all post their responses, and everyone has fun. But believe it or not, you can time-travel way back to those wild and savage days of 1990 when there was no social media or smartphones—you couldn't do that and were forced to live in the moment, enjoying the scene for yourself only. You had to mail your friends postcards of the beach, which would typically arrive at their houses a week after you got home. Those were the days. Oh, how I miss them so!

Anyway, try it. Because what's crazy about it is the effect tends to be long-lasting. When I returned from my trip to Hawaii, I had actually broken my dependence on electronic media. The change lasted for a few months until I was back to my old habits. That's why every three months you want to do it again. It helps break the cycle of addictive behavior.

- **Fifty by Friday Rule: A Maximum of Fifty Emails in Your Inbox**

  My "fifty by Friday" rule is simple: At the end of the workweek, have no more than fifty emails in your inbox. Even given the one-touch process for emails, you're still going have some in there. So try to at least reduce it to fifty. If you get several hundred a day, fifty might be a big task, so find a number that works for you. If you only receive fifty a day, cut it down to "fifteen by Friday."

- **Block 20 Percent of Your Workweek for Two Key Tasks**

  In addition to doing all these tactical things, you want to make sure you're blocking out time to do your creative work. Where is it that you want to take your work and your life in the next two, five, or ten years? You have to think about that, don't you? When are you going to do that?

  To start, block 10 percent of your workweek for nothing but

thinking, planning, and creating your future. Give yourself permission to use time blocks to plan your life. Wouldn't it be great if we gave ourselves more time to proactively think instead of react?

Then block 10 percent of your time to plan your marketing and practice development. If you're not spending at least four hours a week thinking about how to grow and create your dream practice, you're doing yourself a disservice. Always be thinking about building your practice. It's not something to squeeze in when you have time; it's a non-negotiable part of your weekly plan.

- **What Else Must Happen? Get Others on Board!**
  If you have staff at your clinic, or work at home with family around, give timers as gifts and teach others the fifty-minute block rule. Schedule team blocks, since this has a lot of benefits. You probably have people on your team who have a tendency to interrupt you all the time. They knock on the door and say, "Oh, Doctor, I need to know [insert trivial thing here]." We all have to deal with that. Arrange a time to meet with them every so often, such as every Tuesday morning at nine o'clock. Tell them, "Unless it's urgent, save up all your questions and we'll review everything in our meeting." And a funny thing happens: Many of these problems get resolved on their own. So all that time you took for those fire drills goes away. You enable others to become leaders. You enable them to get good at handling the day-to-day stuff. Delegate and trust; this is about giving tasks to others that you shouldn't be doing anymore.

Learn to trust those on your team. Learn to respect them. Have weekly meetings. Again, whether it's your family or the people in your office, let them know what your week ahead looks like. Let them know when your time blocks are going to be and when you don't want to be interrupted. Be sure everybody is on board with the plan.

• **Make the Commitment to Invest Your Time**

Bring your magic out into the world. You're doing a disservice if you don't—a disservice to your patients, your prospects, your family, and yourself. Say out loud as often as necessary, "I'm committed to doing this."

Your number-one action item is to get started! The only thing you have to do is to start. Start with one thing. Ideally start with nailing down your "why." If you can't get that done first, do a few of the tactical steps above.

Start to see how good it feels to actually get control back into your life.

Progress, Not Perfection

Holistic practitioners tend to be perfectionists. We want everything to be just right: our diets, our health, our lifestyles. We look for quality in our food, our clothes, and our surroundings. "Natural" isn't good enough... we want sustainable, organic, unprocessed, grass-fed, seasonal, wild-caught, local, and non-GMO. It is this compulsion to be perfect that motivates us to help others improve their health.

Yet this desperate need to be perfect in order to move forward in your business can be a major disruption. Not only does it halt the execution of your dreams, but it disrupts the overall health of your community because you aren't getting out there to help them. Not only does this attitude put the kibosh on your plans, but research shows that it harms your health. People with a high level of perfectionism are at greater risk of experiencing depression than non-perfectionists, especially during periods of stress and after experiencing failure. Another study demonstrated that the risk of death was significantly greater for people who scored high in perfectionism and neuroticism compared to low scorers.

You may recognize the symptoms of perfectionism in yourself. It typically presents as an ongoing battle with your psyche. You find yourself ruminating on thoughts like:

- I'll open up my practice when I've resolved my own health issue.
- I just need to take one more class and then I'll be ready to launch my program.
- I don't know everything yet; once I do, I'll start to take clients.

Being a perfectionist is no fun—I know this from personal experience. You live in the future, and the present is a high-stakes situation in which every mistake has enormous ramifications. You're under perpetual threat, constantly scanning for worst-case scenarios, always trying to dodge any potential for error or criticism.

So how do you get over this? First, confirm that your expectations aren't completely out of whack. Check on the practicality of the standards you're setting for yourself. The only person who expects you to know everything about everything is *you*. Your clients know that you're human. You're not a walking computer with the answers to everything in your back pocket. As long as they know that you'll find answers to things you don't know and get back to them in a timely fashion, trust me, they'll be just fine. Wouldn't you?

Second, challenge your perfectionist thoughts. Ask yourself the following questions:

- Am I making this issue harder than I should?
- What if things don't go the way I want them to? Does it matter?
- Do I know for sure that things will turn out badly if I don't know the right answer?

Finally, get comfortable with being imperfect. It's impossible to know everything before you need to know it! One of my favorite sayings comes from the book *The Body Keeps the Score* by Bessel Van Der Kolk. It states that "our best textbook is our client." Your deepest knowledge comes not from a class, or a book, or a whitepaper, or a research project; it comes from your clients, who come to you with real-life issues and are testing the real-life solutions you offer. Studying their feedback is the only sure-fire way to learn what works and what doesn't. The longer you wait to work with them, the *less* perfect your knowledge is.

We are a community of lifelong learners. And I've seen people devote nearly all of their lives in learning mode and never get their businesses off the ground. One more program, one more seminar, one more book, one more credential next to their name—all in hopes of achieving perfection.

If you keep waiting until you're ready, you'll never start... and people who need your help will continue to struggle.

Perfection is an admirable goal, but it's just that: a goal. It is rarely attained. Okay, it's *never* attained. Your practice, like your life, is constantly evolving and changing. The "perfect time" never arrives because, just like the horizon, no matter how far you walk you will never reach it.

As you build your power practice, don't give up because you cannot achieve perfection. Good enough is good enough. Don't wait until your program, book, or website is perfect; everything is a work in progress. Aim for the moon, but if you hit a star instead, that's pretty good, too.

You might not have all the answers, but you have many more than do those you wish to help. When it comes to helping other people, action always trumps inaction.

Remember, the people floundering in the raging sea are counting on *you* to be up there on your rock ready to throw a life preserver. If you invest in yourself and your practice, you'll be ready every time.

Keep It Small and Simple!

If I know you—a heart-centered, passionate rebel who wants to change the conventional model of health care in our world—you have a million ideas in mind. And, of course, you want to do all of those things all at the same time! Please. Don't.

The most successful people select only two or three strategies to focus on when starting up and running their practices. Whether that means using only a few targeted marketing tactics—like networking, speaking, and blogging—or creating their schedule of programs or services, less is best.

Few of us have enough time in our lives to get good at any

one thing. Even picking two or three things can be a stretch. Heed this warning carefully, as it's easy to get lulled into doing more and more by the latest health celebrity or marketing guru who has all the appearances of raking in the dough through a multitude of revenue streams and cutting-edge marketing tactics while behind the scenes they're drinking out of a firehose and spending much of that money on assistants and helpers to manage the load.

Get good at one or two marketing tactics for one niche, and promoting one or two services or programs, and delegate the rest to others if you must, and when you're ready. I can guarantee without any reservations that this alone is the most effective and fastest path toward growth, impact, and your sanity!

10. | Navigating the Road Ahead

Not long ago I was teaching my PEACE Process workshop at a university on the East Coast. During that class, a student asked why I was forcing practitioners to niche themselves when their goal is to help as many people as possible.

I explained to her—and now to you—that my intention is not to limit but to expand your impact in your community. The PEACE Process isn't about restricting who you work with, but how to more effectively promote your practice in a crowded, noisy marketplace. You can heal whoever comes in your door! Once your ideal client finds you through the PEACE Process, they will tell others about you. They will have additional health needs that you can help them with. They will refer their friends and family to you. If you choose to work with people outside your niche market, you will have plenty of opportunities to do so through the relationships you build with your targeted market. But to generate a steady stream of loyal patients and clients, focus on and follow the five steps in this book.

I created the PEACE Process using the latest evidence from marketing and behavioral research and through observing (and helping with) the launches of many successful holistic practices, including three businesses of my own. If you are happy with your current financial situation, do what is already working for you and identify one or two gems from my book to keep your patients engaged and loyal for life. If you aren't quite where you'd like to be or are just starting your practice, do more. Make this book work for you regardless of where you are.

You have a standard way of operating with a patient: you conduct your assessment, run lab tests, and then follow a protocol or method to help them heal. But even your best plans can go awry. There are cultural, genetic, environmental, social, emotional, and other factors that can require you to shift your approach. Humans are organic and don't follow a straight line to health even with the best protocol on the planet! You modify and adjust as you go.

Marketing is a lot like working with a new patient. The PEACE Process is the framework for attracting your niche market and creating an extraordinary practice. However, your community, market, style, skill, and experience are all factors that influence how you apply it. Be flexible and open to the messages your patients and the universe send you along the way.

Start with Just Three Steps

You should now understand why your role as chief marketing officer is every bit as important as your role as a clinician. You might be the best healer in the world, but without clients, what does it matter? In a world where there is greater demand (and competition) for your services than ever before, smart marketing is essential. And now with the PEACE Process, it's never been easier. Here are the three steps to start with right now:

1. **Define your purpose.** Reconnect with the reasons you got into your line of work and develop your personal manifesto. Whether it's one page or thirty, write it down and read it over and over until it feels right to you. Be sure to make it deeply personal and emotional, too. It is the emotional connection that makes it real, relevant, and inspiring.

2. **Create your niche.** Using the steps I outline in the PEACE Process and whatever flows out of your manifesto, start to think about the people, conditions, and passions that fire you up. Don't restrict your thinking just yet. Instead, be expansive—dump all your ideas down onto a mind map. Walk away from it, then come back to it with fresh eyes and keep adding, honing, and clarifying as you go. Within a short time you'll have a pretty good idea about how and with whom you want to focus your work. Just leave space and flexibility to modify your niche as you go.

3. **Begin your outreach.** There are many pieces to this step and much of this will depend on which activities you want to take on. Regardless, you should start by doing the following things:

   a. **Create your niche-focused website with an opt-in.** Your online presence is crucial, but without an opt-in to collect names, you're missing one of the most important aspects of having a website. Before you do social media, public talks, or any other form of outreach, the ability to collect email addresses is job number one.

b. **Write your blog.** Content creation is critical for search engine optimization, establishing authority, and crafting messages for broader outreach vehicles as time goes on. Your blogs and articles become the foundation for your book, clinical programs, workshops, videos, online programs, talks, podcasts—you name it. Got an extra half-hour in the day? Use it to write. And if you aren't very good at writing or simply have no interest in it, use the time to learn how to curate content instead.

c. **Make personal connections.** Nearly everyone I know says the same thing: When it comes to driving a steady stream of clients to your door, it's all about establishing relationships and trust. Whether through networking, giving talks, or staying in front of those on your email list through blogging, what matters most in attracting new business is building strong connections with those who believe in what you do. Connecting involves more than just asking others to help you out; it's about helping others achieve what *they* want *first*. Find ways to generously give in order to receive. In fact, if you do nothing else, giving generously of yourself through talks, referrals, or your writing (never give free health advice, of course!) is a game-changer.

Once you've moved forward on the above three steps, you'll be in great shape to make an indelible mark in your community. You'll never wonder about how to position yourself, what to post on social media, where to give public talks... or even what you should be talking about! The PEACE Process is your guide to simplifying and activating all your marketing.

You have important work to do. You are here to make a difference. Don't let anything or anyone stop you. *Ever.*

About the Author

Miriam G. Zacharias is on a mission to help holistic healthcare professionals build wildly successful and joy-filled practices so that more people can find natural health solutions in every corner of the world. A highly regarded marketing author, consultant, and teacher, she inspires holistic health leaders to achieve financial freedom through their life's work. Her rare talent in applying a conscious marketing model to build a holistic health practice uniquely qualifies her to enable others in health and wellness fields to increase their impact.

Miriam has created marketing courses and workshops based on the PEACE Process for esteemed institutions such as Maryland University of Integrative Health, Bastyr University, the Nutritional Therapy Association, Southwest College of Naturopathic Medicine, and the Dr. Sears Wellness Institute, and has taught her marketing principles at a variety of health and medical conferences across the country. She consults with health industry companies and leaders on her proven methods to attract new clients and patients and is the co-founder of the Prosperous Practitioner Summit.

After two decades as a sales and marketing executive in corporate America, the last ten of those directing a two-billion-dollar business division at Microsoft Corporation, Miriam received advanced degrees and certifications in holistic nutrition, executive coaching,and sports nutrition, and ran a thriving holistic nutrition practice in southern California. She has an MS in human ecology from Ohio State University, is a certified coaching clinic facilitator, is board certified in holistic nutrition, and is an award-winning speaker and industry thought leader.

Miriam is the Chief Executive Officer at the Nutritional Therapy Association and President of the Board of the National Association of Nutrition Professionals. She currently lives in Tucson, Arizona, and spends her free time cooking, making music, and cycling around the planet with her husband, Jay.

Learn more about Miriam and her work by visiting www.miriamzacharias.com.

Made in the USA
Middletown, DE
02 February 2021

32961309R00119